PLANNERESE DICTIONARY

A unique and humorous dictionary for planners, architects, builders, developers, educators, environmentalists, government officials, landscape architects, realtors, and students of all ages

Compiled and edited by
Richard B. Stephens

Note for Librarians: a cataloguing record for this book that includes Dewey Decimal Classification and US Library of Congress numbers is available from the Library and Archives of Canada. The complete cataloguing record can be obtained from their online database at:
www.collectionscanada.ca/amicus/index-e.html
ISBN 1-4120-4794-3
Printed in Victoria, BC, Canada

TRAFFORD

Offices in Canada, USA, Ireland, UK and Spain

This book was published *on-demand* in cooperation with Trafford Publishing. On-demand publishing is a unique process and service of making a book available for retail sale to the public taking advantage of on-demand manufacturing and Internet marketing. On-demand publishing includes promotions, retail sales, manufacturing, order fulfilment, accounting and collecting royalties on behalf of the author.

Book sales for North America and international:
Trafford Publishing, 6E–2333 Government St.,
Victoria, BC V8T 4P4 CANADA
phone 250 383 6864 (toll-free 1 888 232 4444)
fax 250 383 6804; email to orders@trafford.com

Book sales in Europe:
Trafford Publishing (UK) Ltd., Enterprise House, Wistaston Road Business Centre,
Wistaston Road, Crewe, Cheshire CW2 7RP UNITED KINGDOM
phone 01270 251 396 (local rate 0845 230 9601)
facsimile 01270 254 983; orders.uk@trafford.com

Order online at:
www.trafford.com/robots/04-2603.html

10 9 8 7 6 5 4 3 2

To June

PLANNERESE DICTIONARY

Richard B. Stephens, Editor

A

a la mode An extra touch to a plan. The opposite of a very common 'vanilla' design or project. *T. Nievez* [See "vanilla"]

abandoned doorstep The original land-sea zone that had supported the port facilities of an urban area, left derelict as a result of the decline of the port and de-industrialization. *A. Clark*

accessorize To furnish with accessories. Example: "The developer accessorized the houses with matching granny flats." *J. Stephens*

Acheson's Comment on Experts [See "expert"]

acre The Old English word was *ecer*. In the Middle Ages, however it was adapted to the Latin of the period and became *acra*, which gave rise to our present spelling. The word originally meant unoccupied country, whether field or woodland. But through increased interest in agriculture, the meaning became limited to land that could be cultivated. And by the time of the Norman Conquest, the extent of that land had become limited to the area that a yoke of oxen could plow in one day. Through the course of the next two centuries that method of measurement was seen to be unfair, the land allotted to a tenant depended not only upon the condition of his oxen, but upon the kind and condition of the soil to be plowed. A good yoke of oxen on level ground and rich light soil could plow twice as much as an ill-conditioned yoke on hilly, stony ground. In the reign of Edward I, therefore, the acre was fixed as a piece of land 40 rods in length by four rods in width. (A rod measures 16½feet.) The practical farmer of those days took this to be thirty-two furrows of the plow, a furlong in length. But it has been many centuries since the acre was necessarily rectangular; now it may be of any shape, though its area is still fixed at 160 square rods or 4,840 square yards, as in the days of King Edward. *C. Funk* [See "black acre," "football field analogy," "Imperial measurement" and "white acre"]

acreage zoning [See "zone/zoning"]

Act of God Damage caused by nature [floods, winds, etc.] rather than destruction by man. Force majeure (French). *First American Title Company* [opposite: 'gift of god' a miracle]

active zone The term is usually applied at a distance. It may connote activities either legal or illegal and/or increased law enforcement, depending on context. This allows timid media to identify a neighborhood that is considered to be a "problem area" without using the exact term. *G. Clay*

Adequate Public Facilities Ordinance (APFO) An ordinance establishing standards for public facilities and requiring new development to evaluate and mitigate their impacts prior to approval.

adhocument Report prepared by citizen advisory committee or other ad hoc group. *R. Stephens*

adminisphere The rarefied organizational layers beginning just above the rank and file. Decisions that fall from the adminisphere are often profoundly inappropriate or irrelevant to the problems they were designed to solve.

Administratium The heaviest element know to science discovered by University physicists. The element, tentatively named *Administratium* [Ad], has no protons or electrons, which means that its atomic number is 0. However it does have 1 neutron, 125 assistants to the neutron, 75 vice neutrons, and 111 assistants to the vice neutrons. This gives it an atomic mass of 312. The 312 particles are held together in the nucleus by a force that involves the continuous exchange of meson-like particles called memos. Since it has no electrons, *Administratium* is inert. However it can be detected chemically because it seems to impede every reaction in which it is present. According to one of the discoverers of the element, a very small amount of *Administratium* made one reaction that normally takes less than a second take over four days. *Administratium* has a half-life of approximately three years, at which time it does not actually decay. Instead, it undergoes a reorganization in which the assistants to the neutron, vice neutrons, and assistants to the vice neutrons exchange places. Some studies have indicated that its atomic mass actually increases after each reorganization. *Administratium* is most likely to be found on college and university campuses and in large corporate and government centers, near the best appointed and maintained building. *T. Kyle*

address Doublespeak for arm waving. "Addressing" does not mean *solving* a problem, it merely means talking or writing about a problem. Bureaucrats and elected officials (BEOs) often try to delude the public by saying "we addressed that problem." If they have actually solved the problem, they would eagerly say so. *Helping Our Peninsula's Environment*

administrative guerilla Professional who works through the system to achieve personal goals in conflict with the organization's goals. *M. L. & C. E. Needleman* [See "Zone Ranger, The"]

administratrix Female administrator. *First American Title Company*

advanced planning 1) "Don't worry, the plans are in the mail." *E. Poventud* 2) Redundant term meaning planning to plan. *R. Castillo*

adverse land use [See "ZOT!"]

advertecture [See "signage"]

affluenza An epidemic of stress, waste, over-consumption and environmental decay. *PBS*

affordable housing
Planner: Safe, sanitary and attractive housing for families earning up to 120% of the median County income, which fulfills a community need and furthers the goal of social equity for all persons.
Developer: Opportunity for a density bonus.
Citizen: An open door for drug dealers, prostitutes, panhandlers, child molesters, gang members, and other people "not like us." *L. Phillips AICP* [See "workforce housing"]

agency anorexia   An agency's loss of effectiveness due to excessive shrinkage through various cost-cutting measures. Agency anorexia joins numerous other diet-related business idioms, such as *Slimfast budgeting*, *trimming the fat*, *corporate bloat*, and *lean and mean*. Associated with it are the terms *survivor syndrome* and *ghost worker*. Sufferers of survivor syndrome are overworked staff members remaining after a layoff, who simply become time-servers. Ghost workers are previously fired employees with critical insights into usually technical operations, who are rehired by their former companies as consultants to perform specialized tasks and solve complex problems. *Atlantic Monthly*

agrarian Relating to land, or a division or distribution of land. *Real Estate Dictionary*

Ahwahnee Principles (Community)
1.   All planning should be in the form of complete and integrated communities containing housing, shops, work places, schools, parks and civic facilities essential to the daily life of the residents.
2.   Community size should be designed so that housing, jobs, daily needs and other activities are within easy walking distance of each other.
3.   As many activities as possible should be located within easy walking distance of transit stops.
4.   A community should contain a diversity of housing types to enable citizens from a wide range of economic levels and age groups to live within its boundaries.
5.   Businesses within the community should provide a range of job types for the community's residents.
6.   The location and character of the community should be consistent with a larger transit network.
7.   The community should have a center focus that combines commercial, civic, cultural and recreational uses.

8. The community should contain an ample supply of specialized open space in the form of squares, greens and parks whose frequent use is encouraged through placement and design.
9. Public spaces should be designed to encourage the attention and presence of people at all hours of the day and night.
10. Each community or cluster of communities should have a well-defined edge, such as agricultural greenbelts or wildlife corridors, permanently protected from development.
11. Streets, pedestrian paths and bike paths should contribute to a system of fully-connected and interesting routes to all destinations. Their design should encourage pedestrian and bicycle use by being small and spatially defined by buildings, trees and lighting; and by discouraging high speed traffic.
12. Wherever possible, the natural terrain, drainage and vegetation of the community should be preserved with superior examples contained within parks or greenbelts.
13. The community design should help conserve resources and minimize waste.
14. Communities should provide for the efficient use of water through the use of natural drainage, drought tolerant landscaping and recycling.
15. The street orientation, the placement of buildings and the use of shading should contribute to the energy efficiency of the community.

[See "rules"]

air conditioning [See "airport terminalogy"]

AICP Any Idiot Can Plan (American Institute of Certified Planners) [See "MCIP" and "MRTPI"]

airport "terminalogy"

AIR CONDITIONING Avigation easement. *R. Stephens*

ALUC Airports Leave Us Confused. [Airport Land Use Commission] *R. Stephens*

AIR CONDITIONING Avigation easement. *R. Stephens*

COFFEE GRINDER Old, unstable aircraft. *J. Green*

FLIGHTSEEING Aerial sightseeing. *The Christian Science Monitor*

FLYING BANANA Build Absolutely Nothing Anywhere Near Airports.

GREETERS & MEETERS For every passenger, on average, there is one person who accompanies them to or from the airport. *D. Watson*

HARD LANDING Airplane crash. *W. Lutz*

INVOLUNTARY CONVERSION An aircraft crash. You convert an operational aircraft to scrap. *R. Holder*

O & D Origin & Destination [as opposed to an airport which is a "stopover"]. *D. Watson*

POPU Privately Owned, Publicly Used airport. *D. Nichols*

TARMAC ATTACK Citizen's opposition to an airport. *R. Stephens*

alley influence In appraising, the effect upon value of a property, because of an adjoining side or rear alley. *Real Estate Dictionary*

alligator Investment property that does not bring in enough income to cover expenses, a condition that devours the property's capital like an alligator. *K. Watts*

allodium Land owned by individuals, as opposed to the feudal system of ownership of all land by a king or ruler. *Real Estate Dictionary*

Ambassadors of the Forest in the Town Urban trees. *F. Hundertwasser* [See "metrowoods"]

ambulance chasing   Endangered species protection. Staging costly, last-minute rescues one creature at a time. Also referred to as 'emergency-ward,' or 'three-toes-over-the-cliff' conservation." *D. H. Chadwick* [See "animals"]

amortification   A shameful or humiliating process (amortization) by which nonconforming uses and structures must be discontinued or made to conform. *R. Stephens*

amusement park A walled city populated mainly by teenagers, who willingly pay to have their bodies and brains agitated on a variety of fiendish contraptions designed to induce vomiting. *R Bayan* [See "family entertainment center" and "facility"]

analysis paralysis Inability to make a decision due to excessive effort to study issue. Paralysis from cervical vertebrae to cranium. *Anon.* [See "camel" and "Parkinson's Fifth Law"]

anarchitecture Anarchic architecture, creative destruction. A city with no planning and with no respect for construction standards. Example: "Frank Lloyd Wright must have thought New York City to be a great example of anarchitecture. Asked what could be done with the city, he suggested dropping an atomic bomb on it." *SlangSite*

anchors away (anchors aweigh) The removal of the largest tenants resulting in a shopping center going adrift. *R. Stephens*

Angry-la A place either in your mind or in a community where either a state of anger persists (as in the mind) or where anger exists collectively within a community. Example: "No matter how pleasantly he's treated, he always behaves, reacts, or replies like a resident of Angry-la." *SlangSite*

Animalcatraz [See "zoo"]

animal-drawn carriage Any carriage, buggy, rickshaw, or similar device drawn by one or more persons or animals in which the public, for a fee, is allowed to ride for purposes of transportation, entertainment, or amusement. *Glendale, AZ*

animals
BACKYARD BEASTS Wild animals that are treated like pets. I.e. possums, raccoons, squirrels, etc. *J. Stephens*
BACKYARD BREEDING Raising animals (often 'exotics') in a suburban setting for pets.
BIRDS 'N' BUNNIES [See "special interest group" and "tree-hugger"]
BOVINE UNIT Cow. *W. Lutz*
CHARISMATIC MEGAFAUNA Intended animals for Endangered Species Act, i.e. bald eagles and elk. *D. Murphy*
COMPANION ANIMALS Legalese for 'pets.' Domesticated animals kept in close contact with humans, which include, but may not be limited to dogs, cats, ferrets, equines, llamas, goats, sheep, and swine
ENVIROPIG A transgenic pig that produces environmentally friendly manure. *J. Baine*
EQUINE Legalese for 'horse'. *J. Stephens*
EXOTIC ANIMALS Non-domesticated wildlife such as bears, wolves, tigers and other wild cats, non-human primates, dangerous reptiles, and other non-traditional 'exotic' animals.
FEATHER RAT A pigeon, as pigeons are just rats with feathers. Example: "Oh, look! There's a feather rat flying over us." *SlangSite*
FURKID A pet treated as though it were one's child. *C. Winter*

9

GENTLEMAN COW A bull. *R. Holder*

GOOFIES Domesticated animals with a trusting manner like cows and sheep. Those who care for them are characterized by predictability, dullness, and a fanatical hatred of predatory wild animals. *P. Shepard*

GRAIN-CONSUMING ANIMAL UNIT Cows, chickens and pigs. *USDA*

GUIDE DOGS/HORSES Animals that assist the visually challenged. *Anon.*

LBJ Little Brown Job. Non-descript bird.

LIVESTOCK ANIMALS Domesticated animals which are commonly held in moderate contact with humans which include, but are not limited to, cattle, bison, equines, sheep, goats, llamas, and swine.

MINIATURE LIVESTOCK Miniature horses, donkeys, cows, sheep, goats, pigs, etc. Appropriately sized for today's 'tract ranches' which are rarely larger than 7,200 square feet. *R. Stephens* [See "barnyard boutique"]

RIVER CHICKEN Duck. *C. Kolyvas*

PRAIRIE LAWYER Coyote. (cowboy) *R. Adams*

RANGE RAT Prairie dog. *Anon.*

SAILCAT Roadkill with aerodynamic disk characteristics. Also "Frisbee cat." [See "roadkill"]

SERVICE ANIMAL Pet assisting a disadvantaged person.

SEWERGATOR An alligator that lives in a municipal sewage system. An urban folk myth. *Daily News, New York* [See "urban legends"]

SQUINK An unidentified animal from 'squirrel' and 'skunk.' *SlangSite*

TRANSGENIC Animal that has been genetically altered. *J. Gillis*

TREE RAT Another name for a squirrel. *SlangSite*

URBANIMAL Urbanized wildlife. Pigeons, possums, squirrels, coyotes, etc. *J. Stephens*

VECTOR Animal that poses a health and /or safety risk to humans.

WNK We'll Never Know. *Los Angeles Times Magazine*

YARDBIRD Chicken. *J. Stephens*
[See "zoo"]

animated space A place in which an attempt is made to overcome barrenness and sterility by the addition of anything that suggests life, especially flags. Example: "Jees, can't you do something to animate that space?" *J. Garreau*

annexoria nervosa Intense fear of gaining heavy regulations and taxes associated with city annexation. *R. Stephens* [See "fear of influence"]

anonymize The removal of all distinguishing characteristics in a person or thing, for example a strip mall. To make anonymous. Example: "This area of the city has been anonymized." *SlangSite* [See "Plan C"]

anthropomorphize To ascribe human characteristics or behavior to animals. The prototype is, of course, Mickey Mouse, but is now extended to virtually all living things. *R. Stephens*

anxiety areas Unofficial avoidance areas. Empty tenement and apartment districts. *G. Clay*

Anyplace Syndrome No 'sense of place.' *S. Kostof* [See "McPlace" and "nullibiety"]

AONB Area of Outstanding Natural Beauty. An area smaller than a national park, but having special regulations. (British) *Parole*

APA 1) American Psychiatric Association (American Planning Association and over 100 other acronyms)

Apartment Dweller's Law One person's floor is another person's ceiling. *P. Dickson*

apiary A place where bee colonies are kept. *Hemet, CA*

apparatchik Flunky bureaucrat. [See "bureaucrat"]

Arcadia [See "rural country"]

architect 1. A drafter with a mission to plan. *K. Lucas* 2. A doctor can bury his mistakes but an architect can only advise his clients to plant vines. *F.L. Wright* [See "consultant"]

architect/city planner *From 'The Van Buren Boys' episode of the 'Seinfeld' television show*
GEORGE: ….Steven Koren has the highest of aspirations. He wants to be (pauses for effect) an architect.
WYCK: Is that right?
STEVEN: Actually, maybe I could set my sights a little bit higher.
GEORGE: (Laughs) Steven, nothing is higher than an architect.
STEVEN: I think I'd really like to be a city planner. (Sits down, addressing the entire foundation board) Why limit myself to just one building, when I can design a whole city?
WYCK: Well, that's a good point.
GEORGE: (Mutters) No, it's not.
STEVEN: Well, isn't an architect just an art school drop-out with a tilty desk, and a big ruler? (Laughs - so do the board members)
GEORGE: (Irritated) It's called a T-square.
WYCK: You know, the stupidest guy in my fraternity became an architect - after he

flunked out of dental school! (Everyone but George laughs) Congratulations, young man. (Shakes Steven's hand)
STEVEN: Thank you.

architectonics The science of architecture; good design in general. *H.F. Byrne*

architectural birth control Limiting the number of children by excluding dwellings with multiple bedrooms. *J. Levy* [See "vasectomy zoning"]

architectural jury Firing squad. *Glass Steel and Stone*

architectural ornamentation
GINGERBREAD WORK Use of ornamentation in architecture, especially residential, which adds to emotional appeal, rather than functional value. *Talamo*
INS AND OUTS Prunewhip designed to replace good design. *M. Roos AICP*
PRUNEWHIP Excessive architectural ornamentation. *M. Roos AICP*
RUFFLES AND FLOURISHES *E. Pomada* [See "architectural style, Painted Ladies"]
SPINACH Excessive ornamentation. *T. Fahey*
WINDOW DRESSING A means of improving fenestration appearances or creating a falsely favorable impression. [See "dress" and "fenestration"]

architectural style [See "real estate glossary"]
AUTOTHEMATIC Architectural style dependent on the automobile and little else. Common to drive-ins, drive-thrus and highway commercial development. *R. Stephens*
BEAUX ARTS Elegant big box design with ornamental signage. *Anon.*
BUNGLED LOAD Weak redesign of 'bungalow' architecture. *R. Stephens*
CALIFORNIA MEDITERRANEAN A 'style' of architecture that incorporates pink

stucco, green trim, tile roofs, and little else. [Alternative: salmon stucco, teal trim.] *L. Phillips AICP* [See "moditerranean"]

CALIFORNIA NON-DESCRIPT Prevalent style of southern California architecture. *R. Mamaghani*

CALIFORNIA RANCH ARCHITECTURE A sprawling, one story, ranch-style building, lending itself to interior flexibility in floor plan design. *Real Estate Dictionary*

CAPE SCROD Fishy variation of a 17th century New England style. *E.M. Vargas*

CRAPSMAN Dubious reproduction of Craftsman architecture from the 'farts and craps movement.' *E.M. Vargas*

CREEPING CRUD The architecture found sprawling all over the urban fringes and rural hinterlands. *J. Kunstler*

DECONSTRUCTIVIST The backhoe ran into it during construction—and they liked it. *Glass Steel and Stone*

ENGLISH ARCHITECTURE A general term, encompassing the styles of various English design, but which have common elements. The exterior being either of large stones, or exposed timbers with large stones or brick placed between the timbers, in a decorative manner. The roof is most often of slate and windows are hinged vertically. *Real Estate Dictionary*

FEDERALE (pronounced 'fedder rally') 18th century mercantile style with a 'south of the border' flair. *R. Stephens*

GEEK REVIVAL Questionable post-modern style.

INTERNATIONAL STYLE No country will take responsibility for it. *Glass Steel and Stone*

ITALIANALIENATE Type of Italian-influenced architecture that does not relate to anything. *R. Stephens*

MEXICANA ROMANTICA Architectural style with a Mexican flair. *M. Brodeur*

MOBILE HOME MODERNE [See "factory-built home"]

MODERN [See "architecture, modern"]

MODITERRANEAN   Ubiquitous style of post-60s architecture with a whiff of 'Mediterranean.' *R. Stephens*

NEO-TACO   Modern architectural style with a Spanish Colonial/Mexican flavor.   *M. Brodeur* [See "house, piñata"]

NOUVEAU-PRAIRIE STYLE   Used to describe an architectural style of tract homes that has a Frank Lloyd Wright look. *B. Inman*

OATMEAL ARCHITECTURE   Contemporary bland, beige, stucco architecture. *R. Stephens* [See "B4" and "greige"]

PAINTED LADIES   Victorian houses painted in three or more colors that highlight the architecture's ruffles and flourishes. *E. Pomada*

POPULUXE   A style that is reminiscent of or based on 1960s architecture and design. Also, mid-century modernism, space age, Jetsonian (or Jetson-age), Flintstone-moderne, doo-wop, roadside Americana, coffee shop modern, and googie.

POSTMODERN   Decorated sheds. *R. Venturi* [See "architecture, modern"]

PSEUDY TUDY   Fake 'Elizabethan' (Tudor) architecture. *J. Green*

RAMSHACKLE   Pertaining to a certain order of architecture, otherwise known as the Normal American. Most of the public buildings of the United States are of the Ramshackle order, though some of our earlier architects preferred the Ironic. *A. Bierce*

RAUNCH OR RAUNCHO   A 'ranch' or 'rancho' style gone bad. *R. Stephens*

RIOT RENAISSANCE ARCHITECTURE   Fortified buildings that appear to be designed to repel attack. *G. Clay*

STORYBOOK STYLE   Fairy Tale, Disneyesque, Hansel and Gretel—these are all synonyms for Storybook Style, a rambunctious evocation of medieval Europe, and surely the most delightful home style of the twentieth century. *A. Gellner*

WOODY-GOODY THEME   Architectural style based on unpainted wood construction. *W. Warkentin AIA*

"X" STYLE 'LITE'   Buildings that emulate an architectural style with only one or a few elements of the original. Example: "There are a few stones along the lower front of that house—Craftsman Lite." *R. Stephens*

architecture, modern
MODERN A blight of colossal boxes that, from the 1950s through the 1970s, mysteriously sprouted and proliferated in the business districts of cities throughout the civilized world, making them visually interchangeable—and aesthetically uninhabitable—for centuries to come. *R. Bayan*
MODERNISM Form follows function. *M. Kahn*
POSTMODERN Notable for enlivening the monumental sterility of modern architecture with a welcome dose of warped humor. *R. Bayan*
POSTMODERN BUILDING How to recognize a post modern building:
Can the building be described as cute, whimsical or playful?
Does it have a big front door?
Does it have a distinguishable base, middle and top?
Does it look like a hat, a piece of furniture, pyramid, ziggurat, a small animal or the rigging for a dirigible?
Does the ornamentation appear to be pasted on the façade, as if all of its exterior doodads were an afterthought?
Are there a lot of big fat columns that don't support anything? Or skinny, silver palm-tree columns that don't support anything?
Are the interiors painted colors that should be reserved for bridesmaids dresses? *M. Kahn*
POSTMODERNISM Form follows fun. *M. Kahn*

architecture student Egotistical masochist with no money. *Glass Steel and Stone*

architexture The Distinctive or identifying quality or character of architecture. *R.*

16

architorture Architecture. Sometimes refers to fad architecture or bad architecture. *K. Moloney*

archityranny The control exerted over us (and our environment) by over-bearing, over-designed buildings that are either structurally flawed (the windows leak, there's no natural light, the air makes us sick) or are functionally useless. It happens when architects fall so much in love with architecture that they forget that buildings have to work for the people who work in them. The perpetrators of this: archityrants. *F. Popcorn*

arcology A combination of the fields of architecture and ecology. *L. Urdang*

arena Thanks to the fact that the citizens of ancient Rome liked to see gory contests— gladiators fighting one another to the death, starved wild animals turned loose upon human victims—the ground of the amphitheaters was always liberally covered with sand to soak up spilled blood. And the Latin word for sand is *arena*. Nowadays an "arena" may never know blood, it may never see sand; it merely denotes a scene of contest—physical, mental, or even figurative. *C. Funk*

arm's length transaction Transaction in which none of the parties has a dominant influence over the other and each acts in its own best interest. *Kenneth Leventhal & Company*

arpentator A land surveyor. *H.F. Byrne*

artichokes Archæological/historical artifacts whose discovery "chokes" proposed development. *D. Hood* [See "stones and bones"]

artisanal use Premises used for the manufacture and sale of items that are made employing only handwork and/or table-mounted electrical tools and creating no adverse impact beyond its lot. *J. Hoke FAIA*

artist's concept (rendering) A drawing of a proposed real estate project. Not necessarily to scale and generally used to promote the sale of vacant land or the leasing of proposed buildings. *Real Estate Dictionary*

asphalt The hellish black substance used to pave the earth so that it might be made safe for automobiles. *R. Bayan*

ASS Anti-Seating Systems. Measure to prevent people from sitting on walls, ledges, steps, etc. Examples include awkward angled materials, sharp edges, spikes, overhanging vegetation, etc. May include signs such as 'Keep off the ASS.' *R. Stephens*

Assessorato all'identita Councilor for urban identity (Naples). (Italian) *C. Landry*

Assumptions: or How the Plan Became Policy
In the beginning was the Plan, and then came the Assumptions, and the Assumptions were without Form, and the Plan was completely without Substance, and Darkness was upon the faces of the Planners, and they spake unto the Senior Planners, saying: "It is a crock of shit, and it stinketh." And the Senior Planners went unto the Supervising Planners and sayeth: "It is a pail of dung, and none may abide the odor thereof." And the Supervising Planners went unto the Deputy Planning Director and sayeth: "It is a container of excrement, and it is very strong, such that none here may

abide by it." And the Deputy Planning Director went unto the Planning Director and sayeth: "It is a vessel of fertilizer, and none may abide its strength." And the Planning Director went unto the City Manager and sayeth: "It promoteth growth, and is very powerful." And the City Manager went unto the City Council and sayeth unto them: "This powerful new plan will actively promote the growth and efficiency of the city, and the redevelopment area in particular." And the City Council looked upon the Plan, and saw that it was good, and...
the Plan became Policy!
Anon.

atelier A craftsman's workshop or artist's studio. *Real Estate Dictionary*

Atmosphäre eines Ortes Sense of place. (German) *T. Sterr*

attractive nuisance Anything on a property which may attract small children and is dangerous to them. Reasonable care must be used to prevent injury to children. *Real Estate Dictionary*

auditor People who go in after the war is lost and bayonet the wounded. *Nevada Nut & Bolt, Inc.* [See "lawyer"]

authentic As in *authentic* Spanish architecture. *Authentic* means an image that we have created in our minds as the way it should be even if it doesn't exist in real life! Not to be confused with 'Neo-traditional' which is a brand name for authentic. *M. Roos AICP* [See "pastiche"]

auto reception area Driveway. *W. Lutz*

autobahndage Tying up city land uses with freeways. *R. Stephens*

autocadabra AutoCAD magic. *R. Stephens* [See "CADD"]

auto-da-fé [See "public hearing/meeting"]

automall Complex of car, van, or truck dealerships clustered together to offer the consumer convenience and a wide selection. *K. Watts*

automobile   1) U.S. Sacred cow: Automoobile. *R. Stephens*   2) "Four-wheel personality" *P. Bedford* 3) A gas-guzzling horse on wheels; source of mobility for the masses, status for status seekers, exhilaration for the restless and sudden death for the unwary. Progenitor of suburbs, shopping malls, motels, traffic jams, BABY ON BOARD signs, drive-in funeral parlors and endless rivers of asphalt. *R. Bayan*

automobile graveyard An open-air burial-ground for expired autos. Grave-robbery is possible and encouraged for a fee. *R. Stephens*

autopia The highway system of Los Angeles, intended by Banham as a place, characterized by the perception of the city. *R Banham*

autothematic [See "architectural style"]

aviary A place for keeping birds confined for the purpose of raising, exhibiting, or selling. *Faquier County, VA*

azonic [See "zone/zoning"]

B

B4 and after Big Bland Beige Box...still. Less than inspiring architecture even with extensive landscaping. *R. Stephens* [See "oatmeal architecture"]

back door The first thing a smart developer looks for. His Back Door is his ultimate fall-back position, should the worst possible Situation materialize. No matter how grand a scheme he proposes, a savvy operator has first calculated the minimum he has to do to survive. *J. Garreau*

badlands Slum or dangerous part of a town or city. Once reserved for wilderness, now used for urban environments. *Anon.* [See "jungle"]

balance The process of making tradeoffs between tepidly enforcing environmental laws and ignoring them altogether. When the Grand Canyon Dam was proposed, every elected and civic official within 100 miles of the proposed dam agreed the "balanced approach" was to build it. Derived not from the Latin "bilanz" - to weigh, but rather from the Greek "balanoc" - to insert a suppository in the rectum to ease irritation, as in, "Please bend over so the doctor can insert a "balanoc" into your equation." *J. Britell*

ball pork (Ballpark, pork barrel) A government project or appropriation with rich patronage benefits) combined to describe a stadium built with public funds for the use of a privately owned ball team. *D. Hayden*

ballot box planning Voter-initiated planning.

Balzer's Law Life is what happens to you while you are making other plans. *R. Balzer* (also *J. Lennon*)

banshees [See "public hearing/meeting participants" and "dock asthma"]

BANANA Build Absolutely Nothing Anywhere Near Anything. *C. Myer* [See "nimbyism"]

bar Age-controlled environment. *W. Lutz*

bark park A passive park open to dogs and their pet humans. *M. Kerr*

barnyard boutique 1) Farm specializing in livestock pets such as miniature horses, pot-bellied pigs, and pygmy goats for city folks. *R. Stephens* [See "boutique farmer" and "animals"]

Baron/Baroness [See "public hearing/meeting participants"]

Bart Simpson homes [See "house"]

basic brown Person who has little or no interest in, or commitment to, environmental issues. *K. Watts* [See "green"]

Baskerville Hall Hearing chambers or meeting room so-named for the gigantic hounds who haunt the desolate outer offices. *R. Stephens* [See "public hearing/meeting"]

basketball analogy [See "sport analogies"]

basketball court analogy [See "sport analogies"]

Bauwauhaus [See "house, dog"]

bean counter Person whose business is to work closely with numbers or statistics, also known as number cruncher. *K. Watts*

beats Regular, periodic, recurring movements. Also, 'runs, trips, swings, or commutes which follow circuits, orbits, paths, rounds, and courses.' *G. Clay*

beautiful building One that is fully leased. Oldest joke in the developer's lexicon. Not really a joke. *J. Garreau*

beauty strip 1. A thin line of trees left next to a highway to hide the destructive logging of the natural forest behind it. *Helping Our Peninsula's Environment* 2. A narrow landscape buffer. Example: "Two rows of citrus trees were required along the street as a reminder of the groves that have been replaced with development." *C. Chipping*

Beaux Arts [See "architectural style"]

BED Principle [See DBTD/DBTN]

bedroom community Commuter community. Also, any community depicted by a TV soap opera. A very unordinary bedroom community is a "white-breadroom community." *J. Stephens*

bells and whistles   Features of a project added after the main functions are completed. [See "architectural ornamentation"] *Anon.*

belts
BIBLE BELT 1) Region with large evangelic population 2) The empire of the saved: a broad swath of land that sweeps from the Confederacy to the high plains, embracing all manner of Baptists and Methodists, revivalists and Holy Rollers, who gather to praise the Lord and dream of a place by the Beautiful river, until a tornado flattens their tent and they dream no more. *R. Bayan*

BORSCHT BELT The predominantly Jewish resort hotels of the Catskill Mountains. Also called borscht circuit. From the popularity of borscht (cold beet soup) in the cuisine of these hotels. *Laugh.com*

DEATH BELT States of Alabama, Arkansas, Mississippi, and Texas, where more convicted criminals are executed than anywhere else in the union. *K. Watts*

FROST BELT Region with prolonged frost

GIN AND JAG (JAGUAR) BELT Leafy green belt of London. *S. Robert*

GREENBELT A landscaped area surrounding a development to separate and protect it from a neighboring incompatible use, such as separating office buildings from an industrial park. *Real Estate Dictionary*

RUST BELT 1) Region with declining industry 2) The aging heart of the republic, now in the terminal stages of coronary disease; a grim northern realm of blackened brick mills and foundries, blackened snow, blackened lungs and blackened spirits; the faded empire of coal, steel, railroads and other industries now dead or wheezing; a province more deserted that entered into, as its citizens depart for southern climes or that great coke oven in the sky. *R. Bayan*

SCAMPI BELT Wilmslow region. (British) *I. Sunday*

SUN BELT 1) Region with predominantly sunny weather 2) A land of perpetual summer that stretches from Disneyland to Disney World, its two main cultural

centers. Now attracting hordes of new settlers as winter-weary Yankees forsake home and history for a chance to mow the lawn twelve months a year. *R. Bayan*
SUSHI BELT Region with high Japanese investment
VODKA AND VOLVO BELT Formerly the 'gin and jag belt.' *S. Robert*

belvedere 1) A building overlooking a fine view. *H.F. Byrne* 2) Gazebo. *First American Title Co.*

berms of endearment
Engineering: earthwork
Geographic: hillocks and hummocks
Landscaping: fine grading
Military: horizontal development
Marketing: contoured landscaping
Common: dirt piles
R. Stephens

betterment Improvement to real property, such as the addition of a sidewalk, that increases the property's value. It is not a repair, restoration or enlargement. *Kenneth Leventhal & Company* [See

beyond the rabbit-proof fence Wilderness. (Australian) *Probert Eneyclopaedia* [See "wilderness"]

bid A wild guess carried out to two decimal places. *Nevada Nut & Bolt, Inc.* [See "SWAG"]

big box retail 1) A very large retail commercial building such as a WalMart.

Emerging value-added mid-price promotional retail. *T. Austin* [See "Wally World"] 2) Coffin/casket retail. *C. Park*

CATEGORY KILLER A category-killer dominates one part of the retail market, such as building materials, garden plants, drugs, or books. *D. Hayden*

COMMERCIAL CLYDESDALE A classification of big box with exceptional "strength and power". *R. Stephens*

RETAIL ELEPHANT A business that dominates or monopolizes an area. *Newsweek* [See "building giant retail stores" rule of thumb]

big boy toy box Garage used for the storage of off-road vehicles, boats, gym equipment, etc. *R. Stephens*

big hair house [See "mansionization" and "house"]

billboard building A building designed to announce the presence and enhance the image of the corporation whose name appears prominently at its top. Structures like this are especially common in areas with laws that restrict communication via real billboards of other large signs. A Billboard Building can be curious-looking because it is not designed to face the access road by which a person actually reaches the office. It faces out on the freeway, where the maximum number of passersby will receive the message at high speed. *J. Garreau* [See "signage"]

biological resources [See "resources"]

biosolids Sludge from sewage. Doublestink created by the Public Relations Industry. *Helping Our Peninsula's Environment*

biostitute A biologist who works for a corporation. One who opens up and converts sacred domains closed to human intervention, into profane ones open to intervention. [Note: The "fact" has yet to be discovered that could persuade a Biostitute that anything a corporations does could be bad.] (Variations: hydrostitute, geostitute, etc.) *J. Britell* [See "consultant" and "SME"]

birdbath Paved area that holds water [even though it was not meant to]. *P. Dickson* [See "hogwallows"]

bird dogging Obtaining the initial lead regarding property, buyers, investors, potential home improvement customers, etc. The lead is then followed up by one empowered to make the deal. *Real Estate Dictionary*

Birds and Bunnies [See "special interest groups"]

Bizmuda Triangle An area which is noted for a high incidence of unexplained losses of businesses. Also 'Developer Devil's Triangle.' *R. Stephens* [See "golden triangle"]

black acre Fictitious name used by legal writers to describe a specific property without a more complete description. *First American Title Company* [See "white acre"]

blamestorming Sitting around in a group discussing why a deadline was missed, or a project failed, and who was responsible. *Anon.*

blandscape architect Minimalist landscaper. *R. Stephens* [See "landscraper"]

blanks [See "lot"]

blathering Interminable, meaningless rhetoric. *Anon.*

Blathering Heights (Wuthering Heights) The raised level or platform in the hearing chambers for the hearing body to place them above the public. The hearing body is, literally, 'put on a pedestal.' Also, 'chairlift' and 'electoral elevation.' *R. Stephens* [See "blathering"]

bleepilepsy: From Douglas Coupland's MicroSerfs: the twitching reaction of a group of people disturbed by the sound of a pager or mobile phone going off. Usually results in frenzied hunting through handbags, pockets, rucksacks, etc. Especially frenzied when a phone goes off in a theatre. Example: "The meeting collapsed into chaos as Fred's mobile went off. Everyone went into bleepilepsy until they realized they had better taste than to use the Nokia standard ringtone." *SlangSite*

blight flight The abandonment of an area experiencing blight. *R. Stephens*

blightning Extremely quick deterioration or abandonment. *R. Stephens*

blood alley Place where a four-lane highway narrows to two lanes. *Probert Encyclopaedia*

blood stirring plan A large plan. ("Make not little plans, they have not magic to stir men's blood." D. Burnham) *R. Stephens*

bloviate v. 1) Lengthy, empty oration. *Warren G. Harding* [See "Public Hearing"] 2) Beware of and eschew pompous prolixity [Beardsley's Warning to Lawyers] *C.A. Beardsley*

blueline stream   The bluelines indicating rivers and streams on United States Geological Survey maps. Blueline streams are one criteria for determining wetlands permitting. *A. Davies*

blurb [See "suburbia"]

Board of Zoning Adjustment [BZA] An officially constituted body whose principal duties are to grant variances from the strict application of the zoning ordinance. 'The exception moves the rule.' *Anon.* [See "ZOO"]

boat livery Marina. *C. Chipping*

boatel A name given to a hotel or motel adjacent to a marina and catering to boat travelers. *First American Title Company*

BOGSATT Bunch Of Guys Sitting Around The Table. An informal description of a decision-making style. *K. Watts*

boilerplate Time-tested language in deeds, leases, and other agreements. *P. Dickson*

bollards 1) Short posts made of wood, concrete or metal that prevent cars from entering an area. 2) The posts that surround grocery stores to prevent thieves from walking off with shopping carts. (Not to be confused with 'bollocks') [See "robstacles"]

bonsai yard Micro-yard associated with a very small lot. *M. Kumata*

boomer The most common kind of edge city, it is built new, usually without a central plan. *J. Garreau* [See "edge city"]

boomerang family [See "demographics"]

boomtown [See "suburbia"]

borrowing Less than a 'taking.' A 'borrowing' is a temporary appropriation by government of private land for which just compensation is not paid. *R. Stephens*

bottle shop Liquor store. *R. Holder*

boulevard (French 'boulevert' from German 'bollwerk') Originally, a 'bulwark' or rampart of a fortification or fortified town. In some communities, an example of etymological history repeating itself. *R. Stephens* [See "Chinese wall"]

boutique farmer A person who specializes in the raising of exotic fruits, vegetables, or other agricultural produce for gourmet restaurants and retail shops in urban markets. *The Washington Post* [See "barnyard boutique"]

bowling alley homes [See "house"]

brandalism It's the "defacing" of schools, libraries and other public spaces with logos, advertisements and corporate slogans. Remember when buildings were named after people we admired? *G. Branwyn*

branded housing The last un-branded luxury territory is housing. Of course, there are famous architects, but they build their houses patron-by-patron. That's the way couture clothing used to be, before designers discovered the financial brilliance of ready-to-wear. We imagine that Frank Gehry, Michael Graves, Robert A.M. Stern and Cesar Pelli will discover what Oscar de la Renta, Armani and Christian Dior realized decades ago, you don't have to be limited to customization. Enter the brand-name home—the world's leading architects, working with high-end builders. Together they will produce limited-edition house plans built to exacting specifications. Architect-designed furniture will fill the rooms, much like Frank Lloyd Wright did. After a specified number of houses are constructed, the plans are embargoed forever. *F. Popcorn*

brew pub A restaurant that prepares handcrafted natural beer as an accessory use intended for consumption on the premises. Also "microbrewery." *Melbourne, FL*

BRI Building Related Illness. *K. Watts* [See "sick building"]

brick-sniffers Renovators and gentrifiers. Also called White Painters. How builders refer to those young couples who, when they rehabilitate an old place, sandblast all the plaster off, right back to the brick, frequently causing structural damage in the process. They then ritualistically stick their noses right up against this brick and inhale deeply, immediately after which they paint everything white except the wood that they varnish. *J. Garreau*

brownfield Abandoned, idled, or under-used industrial and commercial facilities where expansion or redevelopment is complicated by real or perceived environmental contamination. [See "green"]

Bruce-Brigg's Law of Traffic At any level of traffic, any delay is intolerable. *B. Bruce-Brigg.*

31

Brusselsization Synonym for hodgepodge development. *B. Rosen*

BS Bureaucratically Saleable. *J. Hay*

bubble diagram A plan so named because of its tendency to "burst." *Anon.*

budget Spending program computed in red ink. *W. Ballbach*

buffler zone Buffer zone for noise. (muffler) *R. Stephens*

builder's acre 40,000 square feet. (1 acre = 43,560 square feet) *H. Moskowitz* [See "Imperial system of measurement"]

building blocs Groups within the building industry with similar interests and goals. *R. Stephens*

building giant retail stores [rule of thumb] Huge food stores are increasing in number, but per-store sales have been declining since 1983. That's because people are getting fed up with the time it takes to shop in warehouse-size stores. Typically, these stores have 100,000 square feet of food and merchandise but customers start reaching the limits of their patience and endurance at about 60,000 to 65,000 square feet of store. *W. Bishop* [See "big box"]

building height [rule of thumb] A building is approximately 10 feet high for each story. Note: Do not forget to subtract 10 feet for the 'missing' 13th floor on buildings higher than 12 stories. *R. Stephens*

buildings It is well established that "walls have ears" but lesser known that "floors have noses" and totally forgotten that "ceilings have elbows." Act accordingly. (Wrong Shui) *R. Candappa*

bullet-proof Document written so as not to be subject to litigation. *R. Stephens*

bungaloft [See "house"]

Bungalow Bill Tract house architect. *R. Stephens*

bunkum Deceitful speechmaking by a politician calculated to impress his constituents. *L. Urdang*

bunny hugger [See "environmentalist"]

Buns of Steel [See "public hearing"]

Bureau of Combustible and Fire Risks Fire Department. *W. Lutz*

bureaucracy A stubborn clog in the sewer pipe of government. *R. Bayan*

bureaucrat The mole-like creature who enjoys lifelong job security and a generous pension for making sure the pipe stays clogged. The species group name is "a hassle of bureaucrats". *R. Bayan* [See "apparatchik," "red taper," and "terms of venery"]

burg [See "city"]

Burgerdonald's [See "restaurant"]

Burnham Down (pronounced 'burn em down') To drastically reduce the size of the development plan. (Make no small plans) *R. Stephens*

Butler's Expert Testimony [See "expert"]

by-right development Allows a project to be built without additional governmental approvals or authorizations. Developers think by-right development larger than a room addition is no longer possible; they want more. Homeowners think developers are allowed to build anything up to the size of the World Trade Center by right; they want less. Both are, of course, wrong. *D. Ring*

C

C2C Care to Continue? Offer from hearing body to an applicant who has less than a snowball's chance in hell of getting approval without serious reconsideration. *E.M. Vargas* [See "public hearing/meeting"]

cadastral Of or pertaining to property boundaries, land divisions, etc. *L. Urdang*

cadastre Inventory of real property in a community for tax and assessment purposes. *Real Estate Dictionary*

CADD Computer Assisted Deviation and Deception. (computer assisted design and drafting) *D. Hood* [See "autocadabra"]

caddre A nucleus of skilled CADD specialists who train others. *R. Stephens*

Caerleon or **Caerlion**   A gated community "guarded by great towers which rise above the walls." *A. Manguel*   [See "Camelot" and "MPC"]

cahier   A report of the proceedings, transactions, etc., of an official body.   *L. Urdang*

California Mediterranean   [See "architectural style"]

California Non-Descript   [See "architectural style"]

California Ranch Architecture   [See "architectural style"]

Californication   The process of ruining the quality of life of a residential area by an influx of former residents of the state of California. Example: "Damn Californicators. They want to pass laws against breathing heavy." *SlangSite* [See "Los Angelization"]

camel   To act in an uninspired and bureaucratic manner. Based on the humorous definition of a camel: a horse designed by a committee. Columnist William Safire quotes a disparaging remark about unimaginative people who, "afraid of change," are likely to "camel an idea to death."   *H. Lemay*   [See "analysis paralysis" and "Parkinson's Fifth Law"]

Camelot   A master-planned kingdom with 'starter castles.' *R. Stephens* [See "lot," "MPC," and "mansionization"]

camino real   A highway or main road (Spanish).   *L. Urdang*

Camp Cupcake   [See "institutions"]

campestral Pertaining to the countryside. *L. Urdang*

Can you hear me at the back? Public participation salutation. *P. Laconte*

canyon effect A streetscape with walls on both sides or buildings with identical setbacks. A large boulevard with tall buildings aligned on both sides would be a 'grand canyon'. *R. Stephens*

Cape Scrod [See "architectural style"]

capricious value In appraisal, a value based on whim or emotion and not reflective of the fair market value. *Real Estate Dictionary*

carbage Odors emitted by cars, i.e. engine or exhaust, that smell like garbage. Example: "This street smells like carbage." *SlangSite*

carbuncles Buildings that ruin towns. *Prince Charles*

career-offender cartel 1) Mafia. *W. Lutz* 2) Bureaucracy. 3) Big business.

caring capacity (carrying capacity) The community concern threshold. Especially relevant to ZOTs *R. Stephens* [See "ZOTs"]

carnival pattern [rule of thumb] Set aside part of the town as a carnival—mad sideshows, tournaments, acts, displays, competitions, dancing, music, street theater, clowns, transvestites, freak events, which allow people to reveal their madness. *C. Alexander*

carriage house [See "house"]

carriageway The area of road surface dedicated to vehicles. (British) *P. Tutt*

carry kills Costs for the loan to the developer on undeveloped land which may accumulate to a point where development profit is negated [killed].

cartogram The presentation of statistics on a map base. *L. Urdang*

caseload rage Anger with number and/or type of assigned projects. *R. Stephens*

category killer [See "big box"]

cattery A place where numerous adult cats are kept, whether by owners of the cats or by persons providing facilities and care, whether or not for compensation. For dogs: "doggery." *J. Stephens*

cavaedium An atrium, courtyard. *Real Estate Dictionary*

CAVEmen Citizens Against Virtually Everything. *J. Harter*

cave planem Beware of the plan. (Latin, *cave canem*, beware of the dog) *R. Stephens*

caving Staying insides one's home as often as possible. *M. Devine*

CBD Central Business District. The heart of the city. *A. Clarke*

CC&R's Conditions, Covenants and Restrictions. Or is it Codes, Contracts and Requirements? Or is it Constraints, Controls and Regulations? Or is it... these are the legal ridings embedded in the deeds to homes in most new housing developments. They allow community associations—the most ubiquitous form of shadow government—to do just about anything they want. *J. Garreau*

cell tower Tall antenna structure usually for mobile phones. [See "skyclutter" and "telecommunications"]
ANTENNA FARM Concentration of cell towers usually on a prominent hilltop. [See "terms of venery"]
CELLEVATION The (controversial) height of a cell tower.
CO-LOCATION Multiple antennas on one tower, multiples towers on one site…
COW Cell on wheels. A mobile cell tower.
DEVIL'S DELPHINIUM A telecom transmitter tower. Example: "…a grey telecom tower with its pustules of transmitters and receivers, a devil's delphinium." *V. Seth*
FLOWER TOWER Modern style cell tower with arching antennas masts on a tapering monopole.
LOLLIPOPS Short individual antenna panels. [popsicles]
MONOPALM Cell tower disguised as a palm tree.
MONOPINE Cell tower disguised as a pine tree.
MONOPOLE Cell antennas on a tall pole..
POPSICLES Short individual antenna panels. [lollipops]
SEWERPIPE Older style of cell tower that looks like sewer pipers bolted together.
STEALTH TOWER Cell tower that is disguised as a church steeple, water tower, windmill, etc.
SURREALIAN BLUE (cerulean) The blue color that cell towers are painted to blend in with the sky—a color that has never been seen in any sky.
WIRELESS TELECOMMUNICATIONS FACILITY Plannerese for 'cell tower'.

R. Stephens

cellevation [See "cell tower"]

cellular cellar [See "telecommunications"]

center/park 'Center' and 'park' are interchanged to add emphasis. For example a 'sports park' becomes a 'sports center' and a 'business center' becomes a 'business park.' Whereas 'park' was traditionally associated with open space recreation and 'center' with commerce and industry, they are now often mixed to acquire each other's qualities. Almost any land use can become more significant with the addition of the words 'center' or 'park,' but the next level of intensity is often a 'complex' as in 'sports complex' and 'cineplex.' *R. Stephens* [See "cineplex"]

CEQA Consultant's Employment Quality Act. *E. Egger AICP* (California Environmental Quality Act) [See "NEPA"]

certified residential sales counselor Real estate agent. *W. Lutz*

chainsaw consultant An outside expert brought in to reduce the employee head count, leaving the brass with clean hands. [See "consultant"]

chair Non-sexist term for 'chairman' or 'chairwoman.' Also, 'chairperson' and 'chaircomrade.' *R. Stephens* [See "ottoman"]

chairlift [See "Blathering Heights"]

change Four Dozen Reasons Why We/It/They Can't Change: 1) We've never done it before 2) Nobody else has ever done it before 3) It's never been tried before 4) We tried that before—it didn't work 5) Another city tried that—it didn't work 6) We've been doing it this way for 20 [30, 40] years 7) That won't work in a small city like ours 8) That won't work in a growing city like ours 9) That won't work in a large city like ours 10) That wouldn't work here 1) Why change—it's working OK 12) The Manager will never buy it 13) The Director will never buy it 14) My supervisor will never buy it 15) The staff will never buy it 16) The Council will never buy it 17) It needs more investigation 18) An interdepartmental task force will have to look at that 19) It's too much trouble to change 20) Our city is different 21) Public Works says it's infeasible 22) The Attorney says there's a liability issue 23) Maintenance says it will cost too much to keep up 24) Finance says it's not budgeted 25) We don't have the money 26) We don't have the personnel 27) We don't have the equipment 28) It's too visionary 29) You can't teach an old dog new tricks 30) It's too radical a change 31) It's beyond my responsibility 32) It's not my job 33) We don't have the time 34) The citizen's won't buy it 35) It's contrary to policy 36) It's not our problem 37) I don't like it 38) You're right, but.... 39) We're not ready for it 40) It needs more thought 41) Management won't accept it 42) We can't take the chance on that 43) We're doing all right as it is 44) Let's take this to committee 45) The County won't like it 46) It needs sleeping on 47) It won't work in this department 48) That's impossible *G. Osner AICP* [Reasons Why Not] *E.F. Borisch*

chanting In witchcraft, "chanting" is the harmonious vocalization of key words, names and phrases that are used in ritual to attune oneself, raise energy, celebrate success and to become centered. *Roswell* In public hearings, it is the continuous oral repetition of case name and agenda items that achieves none of these. *R. Stephens*

charismatic megafauna [See "animals"]

charrette 1) A final intensive effort to finish a project before a deadline. *P. Hellweg* [See "planomania"] 2) *on charrette* Working one's brains out. At the *Ecole des Beaux Arts* in Paris in the 18th and 19th centuries, students rushed to get their final projects on the school's passing cart, or "charrette". *K. Moloney* 3) Laying on of hands. *Anon.*

chartmanship Chart craftsmanship, the ability to prepare a beautiful presentation to cover up the fact that it contains no real information. Example: "Murray's half-baked proposal was accepted by the board chiefly due to his chartmanship." *SlangSite*

chattel Goods or every species of property moveable or immovable that are not real property. Personal property. *Anon.*

Chi-Chi Frou-Frou [pronounced she-she froo-froo] Shops inside an office building that cater to a high-end clientele. E.g. a gourmet take-out, a tasteful lingerie boutique. *J. Garreau*

childlife reserves Elementary school. *E.M. Vargas*

Chinese wall Beltway that becomes a physical barrier. *J. Kunstler* [See "boulevard"]

choke point Point at which mortgage interest rates become a deterrent for buyers. *K. Watts*

chorography Regional delineation of maps. H.F. Byrne [Distinct from *choreography*, the delineation of map-makers].

churches [See "god squad planning rule of three" and "facility"]

CID Common Interest Development. 1) A community apartment project. 2) A condominium project. 3) A planned development. *California Civil Code*

Cinder City Planning 'burnout.' Also, Charcoal City, Scorch City, Singe City, etc. *Anon*. [See "fire-fighting"]

Cinderella Deal Community arrangement with development for financial and/or aesthetic enhancement. *M. Newman*

cineplex Large-scale theater with many screens. 'Cineplex' is probably a contraction of 'cinema' and 'complex.' [See "center/park" and "plex"] *R. Stephens*

Citizen's Advisory Committee [CAC] A group of local residents, usually appointed by an elected official or city council, who meet at periodic intervals to disagree with each other over the future of their community and to discuss how bad real estate developers are. They produce, from time to time, written reports recommending complicated rules, procedures and standards. Their reports are rarely read but sometimes become laws anyway. *D. Ring*

city 1) Modern center of congestion, noise and pollution. *W. Ballbach* 2) Implies an abundance of something in a given place. Example: "After I had been gone for a month, my house was dust city." *SlangSite* 3) Stone forest. *J. Priestley*
AERO CITY Free floating buildings, steel and glass structures of gargantuan dimensions, etc. *Chashnik*
AIRPORT CITY 1) When an airport is located away from the city and a new city then develops around the airport. Example: Schiphol Airport, Amsterdam. *M. Schaafsma* [See "-opolis, aerotropolis"] 2) An airport city that is in symbiosis with tradition and with the most advanced technologies. Example: Kuala Lumpur International Airport.

Parole

AMERICAN CITY 1) A place where by the time you've finished paying for your home in the suburbs, the suburbs have moved 20 miles further out. *E. Wilson* [See "suburbia"] 2) Made by General Motors, on order from Sears Roebuck. *R. Condon*

BROADACRE CITY Plan for a decentralized, yet urban American city. *F.L. Wright*

BURG Town or place. *Probert Encyclopaedia*

CITY FRUTFUL Combining greenhouses and residential development. (Netherlands) *Parole*

CLUSTER CITY A close knit, complicated, often moving aggregation, but an aggregation with a distinct structure…[that] implies that there is not one centre but many. *A. Smithson*

ECO-CITY A city based on ecology in symbiosis with tradition and the most advanced technologies. *Parole*

HOCKEY PUCK CITY A city which has a population/development curve with steep sides and a plateau resembling a 'hockey puck.' These cities also have the appearance of a hockey puck from a cross-section view. *L. Branscomb*

INNER CITY Slum. *R. Holder*

MEGA-CITY The largest agglomerations of the world are called mega-cities.

PEOPLE'S REPUBLIC OF _____ City subject to continuous ballot box planning. *R. Stephens* [See "ballot box planning"]

PSEUDO-CITY Unincorporated area under county governance and special district services. *K. Sparks*

RANCHO MALARIA Generic southwestern city. *M. Brodeur*

RUMPSVILLE Place where all is automotive and the automobile is art. *Pseudodictionary*

SATELLITE CITY 1) Planned, self-contained city in the growth path of a larger city. *Kenneth Leventhal & Company* 2) A concept designed to stop urban sprawl to the suburbs. The satellite city leaves an undeveloped area between itself and a major city, rather than the gradual expansion of the major city. Satellite cities must be self-contained in order to be effective. *First American Title Co*

YOGHURT CITY Places to live that have active cultures: vital museums, symphonies, independent bookstores, downtown neighborhoods with throbbing street life. *F. Popcorn*

[See "-opolis"]

city attorney/terrorist What is the difference between a city attorney and a terrorist? You can negotiate with a terrorist! *G. Willson ACP, MCIP*

city council meeting [See "Public Hearing"]

city entry fees The mayor of Florence has proposed a tax on all visitors. As the British newspaper The Guardian reports, 'Tourists who flock to Florence may soon be charged an admission to enter the city.' *F. Popcorn*

city trademarks Cities with less-than-appealing names are taking a lesson from Hollywood and changing their monikers to something with more marketing punch. *F. Popcorn*

civil serpent Civil servant. *Anon.*

civilians Neither private sector, nor public sector planning: the general public. *Anon.*

claim-jumper One who unfairly or unlawfully appropriated a homestead, or a mine claim from a prior or rightful owner. (cowboy) *R. Adams* [See "land bank robbery," "land donor" and "squatter's field"]

classically proportioned Traced out of a book of Greek architecture. *Glass Steel and Stone* [See "post-modern"]

CLM Career Limiting Move – Used among microserfs to describe ill-advised activity. Trashing your boss while he or she is within earshot is a serious CLM. [Also known as CLB – Career Limiting Behavior]

Club Fed [See "institutions"]

cluster bomb An unsuccessful planned residential development. *R. Stephens* [See "custard development"]

coal sack Cul-de-sac. (British) *Probert Encyclopaedia*

Coastal Whacked (Coastal Act) Sanity out with the tide. *R. Stephens* [See "gone coastal"]

codebreaking Deciphering or interpreting an obtuse zoning ordinance. *R. Stephens*

cold-water flat [See "walk-up"]

collective nouns [See "terms of venery"]

color code/convention Red–commercial. Yellow–residential. Green–open space. Blue–institutional. Gray–industrial. No one knows where this code came from, but it has become the fundamental planning palette. The rainbow spectrum mnemonic device is 'ROY G BIV' for Red Orange Yellow Green Blue Indigo Violet. *R. Stephens* [See "palette"]

colossal fossil Lifeless structure. *Prince Charles*

columbarium A structure or building substantially exposed above ground intended to be used for the interment of the cremated remains of a deceased person or animal. *Durham, NC*

coma toes [See "public hearing/meeting"]

Comanches coming over the Brazos A Texas formulation of the ultimate Situation. The Comanches were the most savage, brutal, and feared Indians on the Texas frontier. The Brazos River flows just to the west of both Dallas-Fort Worth and Houston. *J. Garreau*

combatible land uses Land uses not capable of existing together without conflict or ill effects. (incompatible) *R. Stephens* [See "compatible land use"]

combo condos [See "condominia"]

commercial Clydesdale [See "big box"]

commercial creep The gradual encroachment of commercial real estate into residential areas. *V. Hodgkinson*

commercial planning kilo-rule [rule of thumb]. Roughly 1 acre of commercial is supported for every 1,000 residents. *R. Stephens*
NEIGHBORHOOD CENTER: 5 acres serving 5,000 people
COMMUNITY CENTER: 20 acres serving 20,000 people

REGIONAL CENTER: 80 acres serving 80,000 people
[See "store-to-area ratio"]

commish Commissioner. (Police) 'Komisch' means 'comical' in German. *R. Stephens*

commissioner When you want another drink—preferably whiskey—you ask for the 'commissioner.' *SlangSite*

common law land Property commonly believed to be owned by the public if they have had access to it for more than seven years [e.g., vacant weedy lots are often considered common law open space or a common law park]. *J. Stephens*

communitarian One who believes that the state of the community has suffered over time as the rights of individuals have been enhanced, and that only when the focus returns to the community will quality of life improve. *K. Watts*

community What every new residential development is described as being. E.g. a "master-planned, low-maintenance, campuslike community." In this usage, it is irrelevant whether anybody in this community knows or cares about anybody else in it. *J. Garreau* [See "Camelot" and "MPC"]

community of 7,000 pattern [rule of thumb] Individuals have no effective voice in any community of more than 5000-10,000 persons. Decentralize city governments in a way that gives local control to communities of 5,000 to 10,00 persons. *C. Alexander*

communutor (comminutor) Community that grinds development applications and/or developers to make them easier to treat. *R. Stephens*

47

compatible land use Tolerable neighbors. *R. Stephens* [See "combatible land uses"]

completion date The point at which liquidated damages begin. *Nevada Nut & Bolt, Inc.*

complex [See "center/park" and "plex"]

Comprehensive or **Master Plan** [See "General Plan"]

Concentrated Animal Feeding Operations (CAFO)   1) Facilities that confine a specific number of animals and meet certain other conditions to the regulations. 2) Institutional cafeterias.

concentration camp   Citizen's advisory committee meeting.   *R. Stephens* [See "adhocument" and "public hearing/meeting"]

concrete cloverleaf National flower. *L. Mumford*

conditional surrender   Applicant agreement with all of staff's recommended conditions. *R. Stephens*

condominia
COMBO CONDOS A building that has a combination of condominium units and townhomes.
CONDO COMMANDO **1.** A condominium resident who diligently watches for and reports violations of building rules and regulations. **2.** A politically active person who campaigns within or lobbies for the condominium in which they live. *J. Holeman*
CONDOMAXIMUM Big condominium. *R. Ryon*
CONDOMINIUM 1) From the Latin word meaning "to share walls with those of

lesser intelligence," it is a legal form of ownership of a unit located within a multiple-unit development. In residential condominiums, this involves taking a large, comfortable living area, dividing it up until each resulting space is too small for habitation and then selling these tiny spaces for an unconscionable profit. *R. Reitzel* 2) Dwarf prophylactic 3) Also 'condo'.

CONDOM The safe housing abbreviation for 'condominium.' *M. Roos AICP*

CONDONUNDRUM A paradoxical, insoluble, or difficult condominium project. *R. Stephens*

CONDOTEL Where the owners can only use their units a few days a year, and the profits [from renting the rooms in a hotel-like situation] are shared with a management company. *T. Binder*

DOCKOMINIUM A marina which is run like a condominium, with each member owning his or her own slip. *P. Dickson*

MONDOMINIUM An inordinately large condominium. *R. Stephens*

SEASONIUM A time-share purchased for an entire season. *R. Ryon*

UNDERGROUND or ETERNAL CONDOMINIUM Grave. *W. Lutz*

condo commando [See "condominia"]

condomaximum [See "condominia"]

condominium [See "condominia"]

condoms [See "condominia"]

condunundrum [See "condominia"]

condotel [See "condominia"]

consensus When all sides of the issue are equally mad at the project planner. *E. Toll AICP*

conservation communities A new kind of low-density housing development in which just a few upscale homes are built in areas that otherwise remain preserved, albeit for marketing not altruistic reasons. *F. Popcorn*

conservative influence An omission error which supports [rather than contradicts] the study by making the findings more "conservative". *Anon.*

consultant 1) Someone who borrows your watch, tells you what time it is, and then bills you for it. *J. Wilbanks* 2) Specialist hired to advise developers on every aspect of a project, the community, politics, and world peace. *D. Ring* 3) Specialist who offers limited services for unlimited fees. *W. Ballbach* 4) Specialist who knows everything about something and nothing about anything else. *A. Bierce* 5) A gelding who runs with the stallions in an advisory capacity. *Private Planning Perspectives* 6) Anybody with a briefcase more than fifty miles from home. *G. Willson ACP, MCIP* 7) A jobless person who shows executives how to work. *R. Bayan* 8) If you give a man a fish, he will eat for a day. But if you teach a man to fish, he will buy an ugly hat. And if you talk about fish to a starving man, then you're a consultant. (Dilbert) *S. Adams* 9. An expert in filling an Excel sheet with random observations, bullet-pointing common sense recommendations, and putting a stamp on a bill because he'll be in another time zone when you are ready to try anything he suggested. *DDX*

ARCHITECT - a man who knows very little about a great deal and keeps on knowing less and less about more and more until he/she knows practically nothing about everything.

ENGINEER - a man who knows a great deal about very little and goes along knowing more and more about less and less until finally he knows practically everything about nothing.

PLANNER - starts out knowing practically everything about everything but ends up knowing nothing about anything due to his association with Architects and Engineers. *W. McDonald, M. Abraham, I. Rufus*

PLANNER - someone who thinks he/she knows what's good for society.

ECONOMIST - someone who thinks he/she knows what's good for society.

POLITICIAN - someone who thinks he/she knows what's good for society.

CITY PLAN - something that results when someone who thinks he/she knows what's good for society despite someone else who thinks he/she knows what's good for society. *W. McDonald, M. Abraham, I. Rufus*

ARCHITECT - someone who designs outrageously ugly buildings in the name of free expression.

BUILDER - someone who builds outrageously ugly buildings in the name of the cheapest quote.

OWNER/BUILDER - someone who designs and builds outrageously ugly buildings to keep off the street at weekends.

PLANNER - the arbiter of taste. *W. McDonald, M. Abraham, I. Rufus*

consulting rule [rule of thumb] A consultant should never charge for less than half a day of work. *D. Corbitt*

context sensitive design (CSD) [See "context sensitive solutions"]

context sensitive solutions (CSS) A collaborative, interdisciplinary approach that

51

involves all stakeholders to develop a project that fits its physical setting, and preserves scenic, aesthetic, historic and environmental resources. Also, 'context sensitive design' and 'Thinking Beyond the Pavement" (TBTP).

contextual Is surrounded by a lot of other buildings the architect couldn't tear down. *Glass Steel and Stone*

contractor A gambler who never gets to shuffle, cut or deal. *Nevada Nut & Bolt, Inc.*

conurbation Urban agglomerations that, generated by forces of attractions that a big city exerts, they invade the whole region. *P Geddes*

cookbook planning Planning where simple recipes replace gourmet menus resulting in gastric ghettos. *R. Stephens*

cookie cutter subdivision [See "subdivision"]

cookies Positive [and more entertaining] concept sketches or representative slides of high quality and romantic community design images [in contrast to negative image of development]. *D. Dahlin AA* Any "treats" in a presentation such as jokes, illustrations, video, etc. *R. Stephens* [See "Four Enduring Questions"]

cop shop [See "institutions"]

copyright trap One or more errors deliberately inserted into a map to help identify illegal copies. *M. Allen*

cornerstone land use Specific land use in a mixed-use development that has the greatest impact on the overall success of the project. *Kenneth Leventhal & Company* [Tombstone land use if unsuccessful]

corporate campus A bucolic setting on which are located the office buildings of a number of different corporations. A Corporate Campus location is equivalent to, in residential terms, a "farmette"—more land than is logical to mow but not enough to plow. *J. Garreau*

corporate estate A vast sylvan location for a single corporate headquarters. The possible number of Corporate Estates in any Edge City is thought to be identical with the number of available hilltops. The ultimate Corporate Estate is the Two Wind-Sock Model. Two wind socks indicate that the Estate is so large that helicopter pilots fear the weather on one side of headquarters is significantly different from weather on the other side. *J. Garreau*

corporate office park The equivalent of a subdivision. *J. Garreau*

costume cuisine [See "restaurant"]

cottage orné [See "house"]

COTU Center Of The Universe. Often used to describe people who are unable to see another point of view and wherever they're standing is the center of the universe. *M. Hornsby*

councilectomy The surgical removal of a councilmember. *R. Stephens*

count to three Working to obtain simple majority (3-2) hearing vote on a difficult project. *R. Stephens* [See "near death experience"]

counter jockey Public information planner. *Anon.*

country ruination rule [rule of thumb] The first 5 percent of development ruins 50 percent of the countryside. *R. Arendt*

coverage The built environment that replaces all life forms susceptible to being removed by a bulldozer. *J. Garreau*

cowboy developer [See "developer"]

cracker cottage [See "house"]

Crapsman [See "architectural style"]

CREAM Cash Rules Everything Around Me. *SlangSite* [See "private sector"]

critical mess The minimum needed to create desirable congestion. *H. Eng AICP*

Critical Path Method A management technique for losing your shirt under perfect control. *Nevada Nut and Bolt. Inc.*

critter crossings Tunnels or bridges to allow animals to safely cross roads. Referred to 'ecoducts' in Europe, they were originally meant to assist migratory herds of large mammals. They now include tortoise tunnels, bear bridges, deer drive-thrus, and more. *Department of Transportation* [See "roadkill"]

croft An obsolete term referring to a small farm or area to be farmed. *Real Estate Dictionary* [See "lot"]

cube farm What most workplaces have become. It's a large open space within an office that's been subdivided into endless rows of cubicles. *B. Fegan* [See "table stable"]

cubicell Cubicle. Example: "Corporate policy allows me to have up to three personal items in my cubicell." *SlangSite*

cul de sac Bottom of the sack. (French) *J. Stephens*

cul-de-sac caves Tendency for cul-de-sacs to have dominant garages used for social activities. Also, 'cul-de-sac culture.' *E.M. Vargas* [See "patage"]

cultura A parcel of land which can be cultivated. *Real Estate Dictionary*

cultural resources [See "resources"]

cumulative impacts Death by a thousand cuts. A single dog bark may not be bothersome, but constant dog barking can be highly annoying. Adding up the dog barks gives you the cumulative impacts. Cumulative impacts are the addition of the same impact multiple times. Synergetic impacts are when two different impacts (e.g. logging and pesticides) combine. Cumulative synergetic impacts are when two different impacts are repeated. *Helping Our Peninsula's Environment* [See "DBTD/DBTN"]

cunning linguist Someone very practiced in plannerese. *M. Roos AICP*

CUP Construct Until Prosecuted. For some inexplicable reason, always pronounced 'see you pee' never 'cup.' (Conditional Use Permit) *R. Stephens*

curtilage The grounds and secondary buildings surrounding a house which are commonly used in connection with the everyday use of the house. Usually fenced. *First American Title Company*

custard development Bland clustered development. *R. Stephens* [See "cluster bomb" and "pablumia"]

customer conveyance mobile lounge Bus. *W. Lutz*

cut-and-paste job A report sloppily prepared from various sources. *R. Holder*

CYA Cover Your Ass, the quintessential bureaucratic precept. Whatever else a government worker does, he or she must ensure that blame for a program failure, political defeat, or other fiasco is shifted elsewhere, diffused, or otherwise defused. *D.E. Miller*

cyberpark 1). A large area of land where computer and technology companies are concentrated, or that has been constructed with a high-tech communications infrastructure. 2). A theme park where the theme has some relation to computers or the Internet. [See "ideopolis" and "nerdistan"]

cybrary Library computer center. *J. Swiecki*

cyburbia Conceptual space constituted from an invisible net of interconnections and telecommunications that substitutes the traditional physical urban environment. *Parole*

D

dark sky preserve Areas that have been set aside for the peaceful contemplation of the heavens, a kind of visual quiet. It is necessary for municipalities to impose these restrictions because of light pollutions, which destroys the spiritual and meditative glory of a dark night sky. *F. Popcorn*

day care center Planning office. *J. Maitland RCE*

daylighting Using natural light to illuminate buildings. Rather than relying on banks of fluorescent lights, daylighting brings indirect sunlight deep into a building, connecting people to the rhythms of nature while providing pleasing illumination at a fraction of the cost of even the most efficient electric lights.

DBT Death By Tweakage. When a product or project fails due to unnecessary tinkering or too many last-minute revisions. [See "DBTD/DBTN"]

DBTD/DBTN Two common vaccines used by planners to "fix" a project they don't like. DBTD is technically Death By a Thousand Days and DBTN is Death By a Thousand Nicks [also known as the BED Principle— "Bleed 'Em Dry"]. *M. Winogrond* [See "cumulative impacts" and "DBT"]

Dead Tree Scrolls Very old environmental documents. *R. Stephens*

Dead Worm Syndrome New Urbanism name for curvilinear and cul-de-sac street design [as opposed to the Neo-traditional gridiron street pattern]. *S. Jacobs* [See "loops and lollipops" and "spaghetti bowl"]

deadline 1) Five minutes less than the amount of time needed, but always attainable with pure speed and radar detectors. 2) Ten minutes if there's traffic. *J. Harrison*

decision support A justification written after the decision is made which gives the decision maker an argument to put with his gut feelings. *J. Hingtgen*

deck PowerPoint slides. 54 slides is a 'poker deck.' *Anon.*

deconstructivist [See "architectural style"]

dedication The cows lost in getting the herd across a piranha infested river. [See "exaction"] *R. Stephens*

defenestration [See "fenestration"]

deja spew The feeling that you've already heard that presentation. Example: "Six project opponents in a row said they moved away from the city to get away from this kind of development. Deja spew!" *E. M. Vargas* [See "public hearing/meeting"]

delayed payment A tourniquet applied at the pockets. *Nevada, Nut and Bolt, Inc.*

delicate detail An expensive architectural flourish meant to distinguish a development from its competition. The structural element that skateboarders invariably discover makes a great ramp. *J. Garreau* [See "devilish detail," "mcguffin," and "Moby's Dick"]

DELLE Durch Einfach Liegen Lassen Erledigt. (German) In English: solved by simply not handling. Leave the e-mail with the notification of a problem in your in-box. Sooner or later the submittor will send another one stating that the problem has been solved in the meanwhile, or at least changed. *SlangSite*

déjàvenue (déjà vu, avenue) 1) An impression of having seen or experienced the same street before. 2) Dull familiar; monotonous streetscape from standardized dimensions and a lack of sense of place. *R. Stephens*

demall To convert an indoor mall into an open-air shopping center where stores have street-level access, and which may also include non-retail buildings (such as apartments). *M. McDonald*

Deminimis PUD A planned unit development having very limited common area. *First American Title Company*

democracy by decibel 1) Misconceived notion [usually held by NIMBYs] that issues are decided by whichever group cheers or boos the loudest at a public hearing. *E. Norris AICP* 2) [rule of thumb] He who shouts loudest has the floor [Swipple Rule of Order]. [See "public hearing/meeting"]

demographic strain Too many people. *R. Holder*

demographics
BOOMERANG FAMILY A household where the kids move back in. *B. Inman*
DINK Double Income, No Kids. "Married without children." *R. Stephens*

EMPTY NESTERS: Parents whose children have gotten the flock out of there. *R. Stephens*

FOSL Feeble Old Suburban Landplanner. *P. Sedway AICP*

LOLITS Little Old Ladies In Tennis Shoes. *Texas Planning Review*

LOMITS Little Old Men In Tennis Shoes. *Texas Planning Review*

NEVER NESTERS: Families that never have kids. *B. Inman*

NILOK No Income, Lots Of Kids.

OINK Occasional Income, Numerous Kids. *R.M. Robinson AICP*

PERSON OF LONGEVITY Senior citizen, elder. [euphemisms for old people].

SENILE DELINQUENTS The growing population of troubled and troublesome seniors.

SIBIHALF Single Income, But I Have A Live-in Friend.

SIBIM Single Income, But I Moonlight.

SINK Single Income, No Kids.

SINK SCUM Single Income, No Kids. Self-Centered Urban Male. *Pseudodictionary*

SKIPPIE School Kid with Income and Purchasing Power. *K. Watts*

SNOWBIRDS Upper-middle class retirees from the American Northeast and Canada who migrate to their retirement homes in Florida for the months of October through March. *S. Mize*

WOOFIES Well Off Older Folks. *OfficeSlang*

YOWSIE Young Obnoxious Whining Self-Impressed Egotist, or the Gen X equivalent to yuppie. *Pseudodictionary*

YUPPIE Young Urban Planner [professional].

YUPPIE PUPPY Child of a yuppie couple.

density The number of dwelling units or housing structures per unit of land [D.U./Acre or dua]. The project I.Q. *R. Stephens* [See "DU"]

density game Knowing that the permitting agency will reduce the project size, the developer must ask for more. Knowing that the developer will ask for more, the permitting agency must reduce the project size. Not knowing if the other is playing the game, both parties must play. This has parallels to the cold war mutually assured destruction theory MAD, thus "mutually argued density." *R. Stephens*

depth factor The increase or decrease of the value of a lot as the depth increases or decreases; the frontage remains the same. *Real Estate Dictionary*

Design Review Board 1) Group of citizens appointed by an elected official or city council to review proposed projects for aesthetic considerations. Most members are not architects or other trained professionals. Had many such boards existed in past years, Frank Lloyd Wright would have starved to death. *D. Ring* 2) Failed architecture majors. *Glass Steel and Stone*

designer The person who stands behind the drafter and hits him/her with a large stick when it's time to stop. *M. Roos AICP*

designer-babble A florid and jargon-filled writing style used by designers and architects. *D. Freed*

designosaur Designer with an enormous impact. *R. Stephens*

developer 1) A contraction for "devil worshipper," and the primary person responsible for providing employment, constructing public facilities, achieving community fiscal health, and building the homes we live in. *R. Stephens* 2) The "Darth Vader" of this decade, businessman who rapes the landscape, who would beat his wife, kick his dog and enjoy doing it. *D. Ring* 3) Cowboy Developer. A developer who rides into town, wreaks havoc shooting up the town promoting his project and then rides off into the sunset after the project is completed, never to be seen again. *R. M. Robinson AICP* 4) A magician who commands shopping malls and office parks to appear on the ruins of historic sites, family farms, woodlands and widows' homes. *R. Bayan* 5) Muscle builder who converts raw land into housing. *P. Hollins*

Developer Devil's Triangle [See "Bizmuda Triangle" and "Golden Triangle"]

developing real estate [rule of thumb] Barring geographic barriers, cities will grow, and grow affluent, toward the northwest. *M. Ridley*

development Whenever there is a flat surface, someone will find something to put on it. [Ballweg's Discovery]. *Col. L.H. Ballweg* 2) Suburban development. The more trees a developer cuts down, the woodsier the name of the resulting housing development. *P. Dickson* [See "Law of Nations" and "Ten Commandments of Negotiating Development"]

Development Agreement 1) Agreement between city or county with private developer specifying the standards and conditions which will apply for the life [or death] of a project. 2) A contract unconditionally obligating a developer to do unpleasant things in exchange for a city's revocable promise to refrain from doing even more unpleasant things. *G. Brewster*

developmental Associated with ignorance, idleness, or the lack of ability. (educational) *R. Holder*

devilish detail The one recurring—often minor—concern of an individual government official that delays or stops a development. Devilish details include bicycle parking, pools, flag lots, and any number of other issues. *R. Stephens* [See "delicate detail," "mcguffin," and "Moby's Dick"]

diameter at breast height (DBH) Diameter of tree measured at four and one-half feet above the existing grade. An arborist's measurement of Mother Nature. *E.M. Vargas*

DIFF "Do It For Free." Commonly heard request. *Anon.*

Dilberted To be exploited and oppressed by your boss. Derived from the experiences of Dilbert, the geek-in-hell comic strip character. "I've been dilberted again. The old man revised the specs for the fourth time this week."

DINK [See "demographics"]

directional growth The path of growth of an urban area. Used to determine where future development will be most profitable. *Real Estate Dictionary*

dirt-eating Druid [See "environmentalist"]

disadvantaged housing Low-income housing. *D. Rogers*

Disneyfication Architectural fad on a community scale. *M. Brodeur* [See "epitome district"]

divisa A boundary, commonly of a farm. Seldom used. *Real Estate Dictionary*

DMZ [See "zone/zoning"]

dock asthma Gasps of feigned surprise and disbelief. (British) *Probert Encyclopaedia* [See "banshees"]

dockominium [See "condominia"]

doczilla Any technical report that should be caged rather than shelved. *R. Stephens*

Dog-and-Pony Show [See "public hearing/meeting"]

dogleg Cul-de-sac with knuckle. *A. Davies*

dog run Very narrow side yard. *A. Davies*

domino parking Parking requirements met by locating spaces on another property, which in turn must have required parking on yet another property, which in turn... *J. Tebbetts*

dormitory town A town from which residents travel daily to work in an accessible nearby larger community. *Anon.*

double frontage lot [See "lot"]

Doughnut Effect
The sugary-sweet outer ring represents the suburbs, where middle-class and affluent families live in single-family homes with green lawns and obligatory propane-powered barbecue grills. Then there's the hole—the city—whose population includes significant numbers of the poor, unemployed and drug addicted. *K. Barrett* [See

"Inner City"]

downzone [See "zone/zoning"]

Drawbridge Mentality A no-growth attitude based on the idea of "pulling up the drawbridge" after moving in the area. [See "growth" and "NIMBY"]

DREG Developer, Resource Extractors or Government. *Helping Our Peninsula's Environment* [See "developer"]

dress To finish or ornament, such as lumber, masonry, a facing of a building, etc. *Real Estate Dictionary*

drive-in corral Multiple food-franchise feeders clustered development. *G. Clay*

driveway 1) Area for parking [See "parkway"]. *C. Atkinson MRAPI* 2) Auto reception area. *W. Lutz*

drop some iron Start construction. From the reference of the use of heavy equipment for grading. *D. Avis* [See "yellow stuff"]

Duchy of Grand Fenwick Any small community with questionable leadership. *R. Stephens*

duck A building that replicates and serves as an advertisement for the product sold within it. *R. Venturi*

duckburg [See "rural country"]

DU [du] Dwelling Unit. Plannerese for 'home.' "D.U., sweet D.U." "A man's D.U. is his castle." ...and so on. *R. Stephens* [See "house"]

dual commitment Conflict of interest. *W. Lutz*

DUDE Developer Under Delusions of Entitlement. *M. Finn*

duress dress Architectural Design Review requirements. *R. Stephens* [See "dress"]

dysautopsy (dyspepsy, auto) [See "incongestion"]

dystopia A locality that is depressingly wretched [opposite of utopia]. *P. Hellweg*

E

e-governance ('electronic' governance) Public sector use of the Internet and other information technologies (IT) for productivity, performance and deeper citizen involvement within the governing process.

earth tones Color palette for modern development that has the small spectrum of off-white to pale brown. However no self-respecting project would use a name as bland as the color, so we have 'Tuscan marble,' 'sunrise sand,' 'French Vanilla" and so on. All of these are essentially 'beige' — the 'alpha' earth tone. *R. Stephens* [See "greige" and "zone/zoning, earth tone zone"]

Easter egg Hidden treat on a map or plan. Examples: "If you look closely at the architectural elevation of the bank, you can see a holdup in progress." "If you turn the map upside down and focus on the stippling, you can just make out Marilyn Monroe." *D. Agnew AIA*

eatertainment   Eating and entertainment combined. From Magoo's radio commercials in Tulsa, OK. Example: "For the best eatertainment in Tulsa, go to Magoo's at 51st and Memorial." *SlangSite* [See "restaurant"]

eatertainment index [See "restaurant ratio"]

echo housing [See "house"]

echoes Designer-babble for "looks like". *L. MacPherson* [See "designer babble"]

ecoduct [See "critter crossing"]

econobox   1) An inexpensive small car, usually imported, that delivers basic transportation economically. *H. Lemay* 2) [See "house"]

economist One who makes an astrologer look good. *B. Thiebaux*

eco-porn A corporate advertisement that extols the company's environmental record or policies. *M. Fischer*

ecopreneur Compound noun from "ecologist" and "entrepreneur". One who promotes ecological projects that "are meant to turn a profit." *E. P. Bass*

eco-turfing Using vegetation and/or topography to establish public/private spaces.

G. Clay [See "turfing"]

Edge City 1) Urban village. Outer suburbs. Metastasized versions of the old bedroom suburbs, grown to include huge shopping malls and office complexes. *J. Garreau* 2) Also called suburban business districts, major diversified centers, suburban cores, minicities, suburban activity centers, cities of realms, galactic cities, urban subcenters, pepperoni-pizza cities, superburbia, technoburbs, nucleations, disurbs, service cities, perimeter cities, peripheral centers, urban villages, and suburban downtowns, but the name that's now most commonly used for places that the foregoing terms describe is "edge cities." *M. Rosenberg* [See "boomer," "penturb," and "suburbia"]

Edifice Complex Powerful desire to build really big structures. *K. Moloney*

Effluent Society Association of Sanitary Engineers. *H. Eng AICP*

egress Plannerese for an exit. *H. Moskowitz*

electoral elevation [See "Blathering Heights"]

electronic town hall The use of televised public meetings to discuss political issues through debate, thereby providing a forum to gauge constituent response. *K. Watts*

electronically adjusted color-coded vehicular flow control mechanism Traffic signal. *W. Lutz*

electropollution Excessive amounts of electromagnetic waves in the environment. *Vogue*

68

eleemosynary   (philanthropic institution) A private or public organization that is organized and operated for the purpose of providing a service or carrying on a trade or business without profit. *H. Moskowitz* [See "institutions"]

Emperor's General Plan   A Plan that doesn't do what the authority figure thinks [or says] it does. *M. Roos AICP*

endangered species: Furbish Louseworts, Wooly Puffs, Sea Snarks, Snow Snipes, and—increasingly—new homeowners. *R. Stephens* [See "urban legends"]

enema domain   Acquiring private property for public use by huge fees and extensive mitigation requirements. (eminent domain) *E.M. Vargas*

engineer   1) There are three ways to be ruined in this world: first is by sex, second is by gambling, and the third is by engineers. Sex is the most fun, gambling is the most exciting, and engineers are the surest [Three Rules of Ruination]   2) The people who highlighted their textbooks in black magic marker. *W. Kulash*

engineer's estimate   The cost of construction in heaven. *Nevada Nut and Bolt, Inc.*

engineer's highlighter   Black felt-tip marker. *M. Schultz*

English architecture   [See "architectural style"]

entertainment x ten   [rule of thumb]   The scale of entertainment varies by a factor of ten. *R. Stephens*
- 5-acre cinema or shopping/fastfood annex per 25,000 population

- 50-acre family entertainment center or mall/cineplex per 250,000 population. [See "family entertainment center"]
- 500-acre theme park or sports complex per 2,500,000 population

entourage 1) The cars, trees and people added to plans and elevations to give them a human scale and make them more animated. [See "magic of miniaturization"] 2) The applicant's project team of technical consultants and lawyers. *R. Stephens* [See "public hearing/meeting participants, planning paseo]

environmental art 1) Geographic scale art. I.e. Christo's umbrellas. 2) Strip Mining. A monumental form of outdoor sculpture in which the artist carves deep parallel ridges into the sides of mountains, creating a series of bold horizontals enhanced by natural chiaroscuro lighting. *R. Bayan* [See "urban guerrilla artist"]

environmental deficiency Deficiency of the area surrounding a property, (environment), which decreases its value, such as poorly designed streets and traffic patterns, a high crime rate, no major sewer lines, etc. *Real Estate Dictionary*

environmental docs by the pound [rule of thumb] Environmental documentation will have a total weight that is relative to the area of project. *R. Stephens*
- 10-50 acres – 10-pound, 6-inch thick studies
- 50-250 acres – 20-pound, 1-foot thick chronicles (The Disney Long Beach EIR was 11 inches thick)
- 250-1,000 acres – 30-pound, 1½-feet thick encyclopedia volumes
- +1,000 acres – its own library

Environmental Enforcement, Basic Rule of From St. Augustine, "Give me chastity and continence - but not yet!" *J. Britell*

Environmental Impact Report [EIR or EIEIO] Long, complicated report that is rarely read by anyone, but provides gainful employment for geologists, seismologists, biologists, urbanists, archaeologists, and traffic analysts. *D. Ring* [See "CEQA"]

Environmental Impact Statement Federal environmental document best described by Winston's Churchill famous remark: "This document by its sheer size, defends itself from being read." *R. Esteban*

environmental impacts Any known or assumed effect on the community, measurable or immeasurable, for which the developer may be charged a fee. For example, traffic impact fees, school facilities fees, park fees. *D. Ring*

environmental racism The exposure of minorities or Third World (Developing Countries) citizens to environmentally dangerous elements. *Probert Encyclopaedia*

environmentalism [See "euthenics"]

environmentalist 1) Someone who has just closed escrow. *M. Winogrond AICP* 2) People who are excessively concerned about the environment invariably turn out to own a great deal of land. There are damn few unemployed and renters in the ecology movement. *F. Mankiewicz* [See "basic brown"]
BUNNY HUGGER A person obsessed with the welfare of a selective choice of non-human mammals. *R. Holder*
BUSHENHEIGEN A German word for persons who hug trees frequently. Example: "They're just a bunch of bushenheigen hippies." *SlangSite*
CARROT CRUNCHER Country environmentalist.
CRUNCHY GRANOLA Natural-looking, earthy. *K. Watts*

DIRT-EATING DRUID Environmental radical. *J.Hay*

DUCK SQUEEZER An environmentalist. From Neal Town Stephenson's novel "Zodiac."

E-MENTAL Crazy environmentalist.

EARTHY CRUNCHY A person or thing with hippie or tree-hugging tendencies; someone stuck in the 60s. In humans, often marked by an abject lack of bathing habits, the wearing of lots beads and hemp, a subscription to "The Nation" and a belief in the powers of holistic medicine. Example: "Jan and Steve could never date; he's buttoned-down Wall Street and she's earthy-crunchy." *SlangSite*

ECO FREAK An environmentalist. (British) *Probert Encyclopaedia*

ECO NUT Someone concerned with ecology and the environment. *Probert Encyclopaedia*

ECO WARRIOR Fanatical environmentalist. (British) *Probert Encyclopaedia*

ENVIRONAZI A person who carries environmental causes to fanatical extremes, such as setting fire to vehicles that she considers to be deleterious to the environment. *PseudoDictionary*

GREENBACK GREEN Someone willing to spend money on environmental issues and environmentally sound products. *Probert Encyclopaedia*

GREENHEADS Environmentalists, tree huggers, etc. Easier to say greenhead. *K. Hurst*

GREENIE Derived from Germany's Green Party and the international Greenpeace movement. *P. Dickson* [See "green"]

POSY-SNIFFER Derogatory term for environmentalists, commonly shortened to 'sniffers." *P. Dickson*

SANDALISTA Environmental protestor. *Pseudodictionary*

TREE-HUGGER 1) Particularly extreme environmentalist. *C. Coutinho* 2) The most common but least serious of the horticultural sexual deviancies, followed in order of clinical magnitude by the tree petter, knot knocker, and serial cross-pollinator. *DDX*

VILLAGE GREEN   The local environmental activist. Example: "Oh, him? He's the village green. He tends the village square." *S. Berliner*

epitome districts   Districts representing non-resident cultures. *G. Clay*   Planned urban themes such as the French Quarter of New Orleans. Examples include: [See "Disneyfication"]
- Butchertown
- Frontierland
- German Village
- Old(e) Town(e)
- Pioneerland
- Six Flags Over Our Town
- Vacation Village

estate   500,000 acre ranch tract in Texas, 3 acre tract in Westchester County, NY, and 1500 square feet residence in NYC. *P. Hollins* [See "subdivision scale"]

Euclidean zoning   [See "zone/zoning"]

euthenics   The science of improving the condition of humans by improving their surroundings.   In contradistinction to *environmentalism*, which is the science of improving the surroundings of humans by improving the humans. *P. Bowler*

Eutopia   "Good Place" occurs when "culture and ecology become a part of design thinking." *P. Geddes*

evil aye   Positive vote at a public hearing that appears supportive, but actually has detrimental impacts to a project. For example, a vote for approval with conditions that cannot be met. *R. Stephens*

Excalibur The long metal straight edge used for drafting and cutting with X-acto blades. (graphics) *R. Stephens* [See "vorpal sword"]

exaction Compound word from 'extortion' and 'extraction.' *R. Stephens* [See "dedication"]

exercise

Activity	Calories Burned
Researching staff report	0
Completing EIR	5
Grasping at straws	10
Beating around the bush	15
Adding fuel to the fire	20
Making mountains out of molehills	25
Flying off the handle	30
Dragging your heals	55
Jumping to conclusions	60
Running around in circles	70
Passing the buck	80
Beating your head against the wall	110
Preparing excuses	130
Saying "NO!" to developers	150
Talking to attorney	300

Dear Mary, The Dispatch

experience economics The shift from the service/information industry to the "experience" industry. The best experiences are composed of a blend of esthetics, entertainment, education and escapism. *B. Pine II*

experiential design Experience design is a design approach which focuses on the quality of the user experience during the whole period of engagement with a product: from the first impression and the feeling of discovery, through aspects of usability, cultural relevance and durability, to the memory of the complete relationship. *MIME* [See "experience economics"]

expert 1) An expert is like a eunuch in a harem—someone who knows all about it but can't do anything about. [Acheson's Comment on Experts]. *D. Acheson* 2) The function of the expert is not to be more right than other people, but to be wrong for more sophisticated reasons [Butler's Expert Testimony]. *D. Butler* [See "consultant" and "SME"] Also, 'dabster.' 3) Someone who has made all the major mistakes in his field. *N. Bohr*

expert witless Not-so-expert witness. *R. Stephens*

extreme makeover General (Master) Plan Amendment that changes the complexion of the city. *R. Stephens*

exurban area [See "suburbia"]

eye-care medical leave When you can't see going to work. *E.M. Vargas*

F

façadeomy Destroying the special qualities of a building during a remodel. [Pronounced 'fa-sod-o-mee.'] *K. Moloney*

façadism A compromise in city architecture whereby, as a concession to preservationists, the fronts of landmark buildings are retained as false fronts on entirely new structures. Developers are thus able to build large new buildings by turning them into a sort of stage set. *H. Lemay*

facilities
AQUATIC FACILITY Plannerese for 'pool' *R. Stephens* [See "natatorium"]
CORRECTIONAL FACILITY Prison. *W. Lutz*
DETENTION FACILITY Plannerese for 'jail' *R. Stephens* [See "rural slammer"]
EDUCATIONAL FACILITY School. *R. Dymsza*
GUEST RELATIONS FACILITY Public lavatory. *W. Lutz*
HIGH SPEED FACILITY Freeway sarcasm. *R. Stephens*
MANUFACTURED HOME FACILITY Trailer park. *W. Lutz*
MENTAL HEALTH FACILITY Plannerese for 'insane asylum' [See "institutions"]
PEDESTRIAN FACILITY Sidewalk. *W. Lutz*
PEDESTRIAN ORIENTED FACILITY Side-walks, usually. *R. Dymsza*
RECREATIONAL FACILITY Plannerese for 'park' or even 'barbecue pit'. *R. Stephens*
RELIGIOUS FACILITY Plannerese for 'church'. *R. Stephens*
RETENTION FACILITY Plannerese for stormwater ditch. *R. Stephens*
SECURE FACILITY Prison. *W. Lutz*
SENILE DETENTION FACILITY Adult day care. *C. Chipping*
TRANSPORTATION FACILITY Highway. *R. Dymsza*
WASTEWATER CONVEYANCE FACILITY Sewage plant. *W. Lutz*
WILDLIFE CONSERVATION FACILITY Plannerese for 'zoo' *R. Stephens* [See "zoo"]
WIRELESS TELECOMMUNICATIONS FACILITY Plannerese for 'cell tower' *R.*

Stephens [See "cell tower"]

factory-built home Surprisingly, a home built in a factory. *R. Esteban*
MANUFACTURED HOME   Entirely factory-built under federal building code. "Mobile Home Moderne."
MOBILE HOME 1) Factory-built home prior to voluntary industry standards prior to 1976. 2) A large house trailer that can be connected to utilities and can be parked in one place and used as permanent housing. 3) Manufactured home that, in adverse weather conditions, is highly mobile. 4) Out of vogue name for "manufactured home." 5) Wheel estate.
MODULAR HOME Entirely factory-built components under state, local or regional code. "Some assembly required."
PANELIZED HOME   Factory-built walls assembled on-site. Life-size "house of cards" construction.
PRE-CUT HOME Factory-built materials assembled on-site. Includes kit, log and dome homes. Life-size "Lincoln log," "tinker toy" and "house in a box" construction.

Family Entertainment Center (FEC) Plannerese for 'amusement park.' *R. Stephens* [See "amusement park"]

FAR   Floor-to-Area Ratio.   The fundamental unit of density, from which all calculations spring— parking, hence profitability, hence human behavior, hence civilization. It is the ratio of the amount of building to the amount of land. *J. Garreau* [See "store-to-area ratio"]

farmette [See "corporate campus"]

fauna and flora An environmental 'sister act.' *E.M. Vargas*

faux gates The gates at the entrance to a residential development that do not close and are only built to give a false sense of security. *R. Stephens*

fear of influence   Sphere of influence. *C. Rangel* [See "annexoria nervosa," "Lebensraum" and "protectorate"]

FECal [See "family entertainment center"]

Federale [See "architectural style"]

fenestration Architectural term for doors and windows. [See "designer babble"]
DEFENESTRATION   A 17th century word with modern appeal. Means "to throw someone or something out the window." As in "whoever wrote that marketing plan should be defenestrated." (There is a defenestration scene in the movie *Braveheart*) *D. Liddy*
INTERFENESTRATION The physical spacing of windows, particularly in a building or other edifice. *PseudoDictionary*

Feng Shui Chinese "Wind and Water". A system for situating buildings in harmony with nature. *J. Train*

feste (or sagre)   Celebrating whatever resource their region is known for from mushrooms to pasta to literature. (Italian) *C. Landry*

festival marketplace An anchorless retail center with a mix of small specialty shops offering one-of-a-kind merchandise, with an emphasis on gifts and crafts supplied locally and food offerings, often located in a unique architectural setting. *D. Sawicki*

Field of Dreams Prime agricultural land for development. "Build it and they will come." *R. Stephens*

Final Phase Litigation. *E. Reid*

fine print, the Conditions of approval. *R. Stephens*

[adding] fingerprints to the gun [or knife] Involving more "accomplices" with an unpopular decision.

fire-fighting Crisis management where people are the fuel modification. [See "fuel modification" and "Cinder City"]

First Law of Ecology You can never do only one thing. *G. Hardin*

First Law of Property Land, once stolen fair and square, cannot be stolen back. *J. Britell*

First Law of Public Land The tough guys always get the ground. *J. Britell*

First Law of Tinkering Save all the pieces/parts. Analogy for endangered species protection. *Anon.* [See "watch analogy"]

Five thousand Mexicans knocking on the door of the Alamo A Texas definition of the ultimate Situation. *J. Garreau*

fixed pie Theory that surviving in the future requires acknowledging that the earth's resources are finite. *K. Watts*

fixes Stereotypical ways of looking at places resulting in the end of a vital visual language and the death of a townscape—when it produces pat visual answers that require no questions. *G. Clay*

flag lot [See "lot"]

flak catcher Public information (counter) planner. *J. Green* [See "counter jockey"]

flash Public hearing presentation flair. *J. Richards* ['trash' with 'flair'] [See "public hearing"]

flea market An occasional or periodic market held in an open area or structure where groups of individual sellers offer goods for sale to the public. *H. Moskowitz*

fleabag area Area of poverty, characterized from the presence of cheap hotels. *G. Clay*

flight risk Used to describe employees who are suspected of planning to leave the company or department soon.

floorplate The shape and size of any given floor of a building. The floorplate that touches the ground is called the footprint, after the shape it leaves on the land. *J. Garreau*

fly-in community A housing development situated near an airport that enables homeowners to taxi their planes to their homes and park them there. *J. Somers*

Flying Dutchman [See "public hearing/meeting"]

folkmoot A general assembly of people, such as a town or district meeting. *H.F. Byrne*

follow the bouncing ball PowerPoint text presentation with a laserpointer tracking along each sentence. *R. Stephens*

FONSI Finding Of No Significant Impact. *California Permit Handbook*

football field analogy [See "sports analogies"]

footprint [See "floorplate"]

footstool [See "ottoman" and "chair"]

'for rent' house [See "house"]

Foreign Aid Federal government funding. *J. Levy*

form-based coding Where the 20th Century Euclidean Zoning model hypercontrols land use—and only indirectly deals with the form of buildings and streets (with little success)—form-based coding deals directly with building form and sets only road parameters for use. *G. Ferrell*

FOSL [See "demographics"]

Four Enduring Questions, The 1) Where did we come from? 2) Why are we here? 3) Where are we going? 4) And, where are the cookies? The latter question usually has the most interest. The Four Enduring Questions apply to meetings, hearings, planning and life in general. *R. Stephens* [See "cookies"]

four [urban] seasons, the Western US: Earthquake season, riot season, fire season, flood season. Central US: substitute 'tornado' for earthquake. Eastern US: substitute 'Blizzard' for earthquake.

four-sided architecture Buildings with architectural detailing on the sides and back as opposed to just the front as on old western buildings. Also, '360-degree architecture.' *R. Stephens*

four to six months Plannerese for "six to twelve months". *M. Roos AICP*

fragging Fragmentation of the landscape with pieces of real estate, space, land, or topography ill-fitted for future human uses. *G. Clay*

freeway 1) What ties communities together. *R. Castillo* 2) A clogged artery that connects suburbia with the real world, enabling its mild-mannered residents to shout invigorating oaths, use colorful hand gestures and run their neighbors off the road in preparation for another day at the office. *R. Bayan* [See "facilities"]

freeway prophecy (circa 1950) "Eight lanes of shimmering cement running from here to Pasadena! I see a place where people get on and off the freeway, off and on, off and on, all day and all night... I see a street of gas stations, inexpensive motels, restaurants that serve rapidly prepared food, tire salons, automobile dealerships, and wonderful, wonderful billboards as far as the eye can see. My God, it'll be beautiful!"

Judge Doom, the cartoon villain of the movie 'Who Framed Roger Rabbit?'

frequent flyer [See "public hearing/meeting participants"]

Friction Factor The path of most resistance. The notion is that the degree of difficulty of getting from one place to another, by whatever means, can be calculated and used to predict the paths people will take. *J. Garreau*

FRISBEE [See "institutions"]

frontage The front part of a lot as opposed to the back of a lot or "backage." In very wealthy areas, it is pronounced similar to the word "montage." *C. Chipping*

frozen dessert vending vehicle Plannerese for "ice cream truck/van." *C. Chipping*

fructus industriales Those things created by the labor (industry) of man rather than by nature alone. For example: a planted crop rather than an iron ore deposit. Important because Fructus Industriales is treated as personal property. [See "fructus naturales"] *Real Estate Dictionary*

fructus naturales Produced by nature alone, such as trees (not planted by man), or minerals in the ground. Considered real property. [See "fructus industriales"] *Real Estate Dictionary*

fuel modification 1) Alteration of environment in the vicinity of project to inhibit fire hazard. 2) Euphemism for CYA. [See "CYA"]

functionality Plannerese for "function". *M. Roos AICP*

funding Money from the government. *T. Sowell*

G

Gagplanistan A place of massively meaningless planning. *L. Northrup*

Gaia (Greek goddess of the Earth) The entire range of living matter on Earth, from whales to viruses, can be regarded as a single entity, capable of manipulating its environment to suit its needs. *J. Lovelock*

Gangri-la Hoodlum city paradise. The 'hood.' *R. Stephens*

garage lodge Garage conversion. *R. Stephens* [See "big boy toy box," "cul-de-sac caves" and "patage"]

garage mahal A large or opulent garage or parking structure. *C. Quinnell*

garbage garage The transitional area of a house between living space and the dump, occasionally shared by a car. *C. Chipping*

garden ecology View of nature as a 'garden' to be managed summarized by Goethe as 'our earthly ball a people garden.' *W. von Goethe* [See "zoo"]

garden of remembrance The curtilage of a crematorium. *R. Holder* [See "curtilage"]

gated community An enclave of housing [community is a misnomer] common to conventional suburban development that is surrounded partially or entirely by a wall and accessed by a single vehicular entrance which may be guarded. The putative purpose of this is to provide security but it is usually provided only as a promotional device. *G. Stern* [See "privatopia"]

gater Person who lives in a gated community. *S. Whitney*

gavel-to-gavel Period from the opening to the adjournment of a public hearing. *R. Stephens* [See "public hearing"]

gazinda A street whose name changes depending on how far along the street you are. Example: "If you had trouble finding the store it's because Benton street is a gazinda; you start down Lower Muscatine, and that goes into Kirkwood, which goes into Benton." (goes into) *SlangSite*

Geek Revival [See "architectural style"]

General Flan (California) [Master Flan] The relatively bland, custard-like filling in many General Plans. *R. Stephens*

General Plan (California) [Master Plan] 1) A legal document in the form of a map and accompanying text adopted by the local legislative body. The plan is a compendium of its policies regarding the long-term development of its jurisdiction. It is sometimes called a city plan, comprehensive plan, or master plan, and it may be neither urban, comprehensive, masterful, general nor a plan. *J. Freiman* 2) The 'Mother of All Plans.' *R. Stephens* 3) Either a very good door stop or job security for photocopier repair-people [not to mention planners]! *Dear Mary in "The Dispatch"* 4) A picture of Utopia; an unfulfilled subconscious desire; planner's talk for libido. *R.*

General Plan Prospectus (California) [Master Plan Update] A General Plan Update document for public review. *R. Stephens*

generica The stores and strip malls you can see in any town in America. They all look the same (generic). Example: "When you see anything in a town that looks the same as in any other town in America you just comment generica." *M. Suna*

genetic cul-de-sac A place showing signs of inbreeding. *PseudoDictionary*

gentrification 1) The deliberate transformation of a dull or seedy neighborhood into a pretentious one, so as to attract a better class of pedestrian. *R. Bayan* ['gentrifugal force'] 2) Property improvement that leads to bringing a more prosperous group into a building or a neighborhood. The term has different connotations to different people, depending on whether one has the money to buy in (the gentry) or is forced to move out (the displaced). *D.E. Miller*

geoflatus The foul smell produced by oil refineries and pump jacks usually on a regular basis, especially around West Texas. *J. Duckering* [See "scents of place"]

geomancy Public official decision-making from indecipherable maps and plans. (A system of divination involving the interpretation of lines and figures) *R. Stephens*

gerbil tube A glass-enclosed pedestrian overpass connecting two buildings. *R. Campbell*

gerrymander To divide an area into districts, against the obvious natural divisions, in order to accomplish an unlawful purpose. For example: To divide a school district to keep out certain people for reasons of race or religion; to divide a political voting district as to give power to a political party. *Real Estate Dictionary*

ghetto 1) An isolated enclave populated by kindred types who would be made to feel unwelcome outside its boundaries; e.g., blacks in 1920s Harlem, Jews in 1930s Warsaw, women in secretarial pool, or a class of honor students at an urban high school. *R. Bayan* 2) Substandard housing. 3) Inner city. 4) Rough-and-tumble neighborhood. *W. Lutz* [See "inner city" and "squatter settlements"]

ghettoizing Non-integration of low-cost housing into a mixed-income program resulting in ghettos. *B. Inman*

ghost worker [See "agency anorexia"]

gingerbread work [See "architectural ornamentation"]

giraffiti Graffiti painted in a very high spot. *R. Grove* [See "graffiti"]

global sourcing Outsourcing. The procuring of services from a supplier outside the U.S. in order to cut costs. Also, 'global resources'. *C. Aguilar*

glocal Global and local simultaneously. *M. Schrenk*

glossolalia Glossing over in Plannerese. *C. Chipping* [See "speaking in tongues"]

gobbler's knob A high hill, usually the most prominent in the area. *PseudoDictionary*

god squad planning rule of three [rule of thumb] Three 3-acre churches may be supported for every 5,000 population. *R. Stephens*

God's green acres [See "zone/zoning"]

golden age ghetto [See "NORC"]

golden ghetto An urban area with an above-average concentration of high-end stores and affluent housing; any prosperous area or situation. *B. Came*

Golden Key, The [See "Magic Phrase"]

Golden Rule of Planning If the project proposed is consistent with the community expectations the mechanisms for approval will be obtained. If the project proposed is inconsistent with the community expectations... *W. H. Claire III AICP*

Golden Triangle, The A place claimed to be especially development-worthy because of its location at the confluence of three roads. At extreme levels, reference is made to the Platinum Triangle. *J. Garreau* [See "Bizmuda Triangle"]

goldplating 1) Oversizing infrastructure. *P. Bedford* 2) Excessive bureaucratic regulation and enforcement. *R. Holder*

golf course standard [rule of thumb] The standard golf course requires nine acres per hole or 162 acres. The championship golf course requires 10 acres per hole or 180 acres. *R. Stephens*

Golf Course Syndrome Locating facilities at the whim of the property owner. *D.*

GONADS   Graphic, Organization, Name, Arrow, Date, Scale. Map or plan components. (cartography) *A. Davies*

gone coastal Walking on the edge between harmless insanity and violent behavior. Example: "That commissioner went coastal and demanded a seashell inventory." (Postal) *R. Stephens* [See "Coastal Whacked"]

gone native Public sector planner who takes a job in the private sector. *R. Stephens* [See "seeing the light" and "turning to the dark side"]

good dirt An investment-worthy location. *J. Garreau*

GORK God only really knows. *P. Carolin* [from the medical diagnosis "G.O.K."]

government System of control over many people who, individually, cannot control themselves. *W. Ballbach*

governmental relations Bribery of coercion. *R. Holder*

grade, maximum recommended [rule of thumb] Generally, commercial vehicles cannot negotiate a gradient of 12 per cent or more in freezing conditions unless some method of de-icing (such as salting, gritting or road surface heating by buried cables) is used. *P. Tutt*

grading
BALANCED GRADING   Sandbox approach to grading: no dirt is brought in

89

(imported) or sent out (exported).

CONTOUR GRADING Sculpture approach: the final development has a natural appearance.

CUSTOM PAD GRADING The land is graded only enough to accommodate streets and buildings.

EARTHWORK User-friendly term for 'grading.'

GRADING ON THE CURVE Contour grading.

MASS GRADING The mother of all grading: everything is leveled.

SUPER PAD GRADING McGrading: rather than individual pads, large pads are graded to accommodate many buildings.

TERRACE GRADING Machu Picchu approach: large pads that create hillside terraces.

R. Stephens

graffiti 1) Urban Scrawl; the rude calligraphy of the streets, apt to embellish any wall, statue, subway car or wino within reach of a spray can. Reassuring evidence that today's youth retain a passing acquaintance with the written word. *R. Bayan* 2) Visual terrorism. [See "tagger"] 3) Art Crime. *H. Hahn* [See "giraffiti"]

Grand Dame [See "house"]

Grandfather Clause The clause in a law permitting the continuation of a use, business, etc., which, when established, was permissible but, because of a change in the law, is now not permissible. *First American Title Co.*

Grandmother Principle on Ethics [rule of thumb] Use your head, and ask yourself, 'What your grandmother would think if she knew of your actions?' *D. Hageman*

granny flat / annex A renovation or addition to a residence, which is meant to house an elderly relative. *Probert Encyclopaedia* [See "house, echo housing"]

grant gnats People who earn their living securing federal and state housing funds. *B. Inman*

graphic [noun] Plannerese for "picture" most common in plural form. The term "graphics" in this use is less 'artistic' and hence, more 'scientific' than "pictures", "sketches", "renderings" or "illustrations". Additional precision points for "graphic representation" and 'ooh ah' value for "artist's concept". In some circles, "visual aids" is the *nom du jour*. *R. Stephens* [see "cookies"]

graphicity   The quality of being extremely graphic (visually, verbally). *PseudoDictionary*

green
"GO GREEN" A firm or agency taking environmentally conscious action, such as recycling programs.   *McDonald's* and *Chief Auto Parts* have "gone green" [environment friendly].
GREEN GRAVEYARD Golf course. Wholesale destruction and removal of existing habitat and food chain and its continuous use of pesticides to kill all native species. *Helping Our Peninsula's Environment*
GREEN INFRASTRUCTURE   A local, regional or national, natural life support system—an interconnected network of protected land and water that supports native species, maintains natural ecological processes, sustains air and water resources and contributes to the health and quality of life.
GREENBACK GREEN [See "environmentalist"]
GREENBELT   Contemporary landscape version of medieval moat where city

dwellers are separated from suburbarian settlements. It is a difference of opinion who is protected from whom. *R. Stephens*

GREENFIELD A project developed on raw land. [See "brownfield"]

GREENHEAD [See "environmentalist"]

GREENHOUSE EFFECT Global warming due to the increase of greenhouse gases. Everybody is doing something about the weather, but nobody's talking about it. *J. Harte*

GREENIES [See "environmentalist"]

GREENLOCK [See "-lock"]

GREENSCAMMING Giving environmentally friendly names to groups or products that have little or nothing to do with the environment. *Word Spy*

GREENWASH The process of touting the environmental benefits of a product or policy in order to deflect attention from other less savory aspects. *J. Mauro*

NOM DE GREEN Organizational name implying environmental consciousness.

RE-GREEN To restore an area that has suffered environmental damage. *L. Duan*

SOYLENT GREEN Extreme environmental policies. *R. Stephens*

greige The otherwise inexplicable color of office cubicles and walls. An unknown mixture of gray and beige. *A. Christ* Also, 'PC putty' and 'splooge' prison oatmeal. [See "earth tones"]

gridlock [See "-lock"]

Grimm A disgruntled city planner. From the character Grimm in the film "Quick Change." The clown is in fact a bank robber named Grimm, played by Bill Murray as a disgruntled city planner who has decided to pull off the perfect heist and get out of town. *R. Ebert*

92

Grimoire   General/Master Plan. This is the book of magical spells and techniques designed to act as a guide for the planner. *Roswell* [See "property owner's manual"]

ground truthing   A pompous term to describe the age old art of getting out of the office and into the field to see what is actually out there. In simpler times called 'field checking.' *N. Williams AICP*

groundscraper   Building that hugs the earth. *C. Jencks*

growth
NO GROWTH A belief that no further building should be permitted anywhere until all existing problems have been solved: traffic, air pollution, sewage, solid waste, gang warfare, and nuclear weapons. Usually held by a homeowner who thinks the last truly justified construction project was the building of his house.
SLOW GROWTH Somewhere between controlled and no growth.
REASONABLE GROWTH Somewhere between controlled and slow growth.
CONTROLLED GROWTH Belief that calls for regulation while permitting additional construction. Generally held by elected officials and parents whose grown children can't move out because they can't find affordable housing.
DIRECTIONAL GROWTH The path of growth of an urban area. Used to determine where future development will be most profitable. *Real Estate Dictionary*
REGULATED GROWTH Belief that all projects should be approved, but only after extensive study, public hearings, and complicated negotiations. Opposed by both homeowners and developers but heavily supported by the consultants who are hired for the studies and negotiations.
PRO-GROWTH Belief that construction should be regulated by the free market, and that building, safety, and zoning codes are communist plots. *D. Ring*
MALIGNANT No-growth diagnosis

BENEVOLENT Pro-growth diagnosis
SMART GROWTH The better alternative.

Gucci gulch [See "special interest lobby"]

GUD Geographically UnDesirable. *S. Howard*

guerilla suburbia Area where the forces of city expansion run strongest, where country is in full retreat. *G. Clay*

gun monkey Person who operates surveying equipment generally has little knowledge of land surveying other than pushing buttons. Example: Bruce's resume listed his occupation as "survey technician," but he was really just a plain ole gun monkey. *T. Evans*

gunslinger [See "hired gun"]

gymnacafetorium A large room usually found in modern schools and churches. It can be used as a gymnasium, cafeteria and an auditorium (though not all three at the same time.) *PseudoDictionary*

H

hacked map Poorly designed subdivision (tract) map. *R. Stephens*

hairpin marking A double-painted line separating parking stalls. *H. Moskowitz*

handout A written or printed statement issued publicly containing tendentious information. *R. Holder*

handyman special A derelict building. *R. Holder*

Hanlon's Razor Never attribute to malice that which can be adequately explained by stupidity. *G. Harris*

haphazardous materials Urban litter. *J. Stephens*

Happy Talk All the things in the development business that are almost real. *M. Roos AICP*

Haz Maniacs The special crew that handles hazardous materials. *J. Nash*

hazmat Hazardous Materials. I.e. poisons, toxic gases, acids, explosives, chili dogs, etc. *C. Bright* [See "RHYTHM"]

headache bars The horizontal pipes over the entrance to parking garages meant to prevent large vehicles from entering. *J. Garreau*

health, safety and welfare Planning mantra for the foundation of all decision-making. Planning 'prime directive.' *E.M. Vargas*

hearing body language The non-verbal communication of the hearing body including the space and elevation from the public, posture, facial expressions, etc. *R. Stephens* [See "Blathering Heights"]

hearing groupie [See "public hearing/meeting participants"]

hearing hammer Gavel. Also, 'meeting mallet.' *R. Stephens*

Hearing from Hell [See "public hearing/meeting"]

heat island An area, such as a city or industrial site, having consistently higher temperatures than surrounding areas because of a greater retention of heat, as by buildings, concrete, and asphalt. *Dictionary.com*

hegemony Sphere of influence. *PseudoDictionary* [See "fear of influence"]

height density A zoning term referring to the regulation of maximum building heights for structures in given areas. *Real Estate Dictionary*

Heinrich Maneuver Preapplication approval requested of City Council by land owner named Heinrich. *M. Roos AICP*

Hekawi Tribe [See "public hearing/meeting participant"]

heterogeneous An appraisal term describing an area composed of buildings of varied styles or uses. Not as desirable as homogeneous property. *Real Estate Dictionary* [See "homogeneous"]

highest and best use 1) Appraisal term referring to the reasonable and probable use of a property that will produce the highest return over a given period of time. *Kenneth Leventhal & Company* 2) High Density Residential and/or Commercial uses. No others need apply. *M. Roos AICP* 3) Whatever the person wants to do with the property. (appraisal).

hippodamist A city planner [from Hippodamus, a fifth-century Greek architect, who planned the first city]. *H.F. Byrne*

hired gun Professional consultant [typically well-known and expensive] used to acquire desired results in difficult situations. The term 'hired gun' adds a sinister tone to 'contract planner.' Also 'gunslinger.' *R. Stephens* [See "consultant"]

historic district A cluster of gracious old buildings permitted to survive as long as they can generate more revenue than the convention center proposed for the same site. *R. Bayan*

historic preservation The President once used their bathroom or his dog 'used' their front lawn. *R. Castillo* [See "hysteric preservation"]

hobo jungle Shanty town. [See "jungle"]

hockey puck city [See "city"]

hogwallows Small depressions formed by heavy rains, resembling the depressions left after the wallowing of hogs. *Real Estate Dictionary* [See "birdbath"]

Hollywood parking [See "parking"]

homesite [See "lot"]

home zone [See "zone/zoning"]

homeowner In the eyes of some beholders, a member of an irrational, irresponsible, and shortsighted mob whose goals include unemployment, unaffordable housing, and rolling back our lifestyle to caveman days. Also the person we see in the mirror when a developer proposes a major project in our neighborhood. *D. Ring*

homogeneous Similar or the same. In appraisal, an area having similar style properties or properties of similar use is considered more valuable than a heterogeneous area. *Real Estate Dictionary* [See "heterogeneous"]

hood Urban slang for 'neighborhood.' [See "Gangri-la" and "nabe"]

horsiculture The culture of a town designed specifically for horse ownership—with large parcels, stables everywhere, and few paved roads. e.g., The horsiculture of Norco, CA, is clearly evidenced by the fact that they have a hitching post outside of the town's McDonald's restaurant. *PseudoDictionary*

hospital size [rule of thumb] Four beds per thousand population. *P. Tutt*

hotel rule of three [rule of thumb] The third owner of a hotel will make a profit. By that time, the cost of the building will reflect its true market value. *D. Meengs*

house
ANIMAL HOUSE Fraternity house.
ARFENHOUSE A mansion-sized house with only one room. Tends to be high in property value for no reason whatsoever. *SlangSite* [See "mansionization"]
BART SIMPSON HOMES Homes that have castle-like architecture. *B. Inman*
BAUWAUHAUS Functionally designed, but esthetically dismal house; a dog. *R.*

98

BIG HAIR HOUSE [See "mansionization"]

BOWLING ALLEY HOUSES Homes developed on long, narrow lots, so that most rooms are lined up along a single hallway extending from the front of the home to the rear. *L. Phillips AICP* [See "sausage homes"]

BULL'S MANSH Main house on a ranch. From 'bull's mansion.' (cowboy) *R. Adams*

BUNGALOFT A bungalow style house that also has a loft. *M. Davie*

CARRIAGE HOUSE A single-family home with a second unit on the garage. *B. Inman*

COTTAGE ORNÉ Pseudo-medieval farmhouse. *J. Kunstler*

CRACKER COTTAGE Southern wood-framed dwelling with deep roof overhangs, ample windows, and a broad porche. *J. Kunstler*

CRIB 'House' in the 'hood.

DERRY Derelict house, especially one used by tramps, drug addicts, etc. (British) *Anon.* [See "handyman special"]

DES RES Desirable residence. *Probert Encyclopaedia*

EARTHSHIP An environmentally self-sufficient house powered by renewable energy sources and partially made from used tires and recyclable materials. *High Mesa Foundation*

ECHO HOUSING A small, removable modular cottage on a concrete foundation or slab in the rear or side yard of a dwelling. Comment: Echo housing is also known as a "granny" flat or elder cottage housing. *H. Moskowitz* [See "granny flat"]

ECONOBOX A small, inexpensive home. *R. Esteban*

ELDER COTTAGE HOUSING [See "house, echo housing"]

EXPANSIBLE HOUSE A house specifically designed for additions or later expansion. *Real Estate Dictionary*

FACTORY-BUILT HOME [See "factory-built home"]

'FOR RENT' HOUSE Apartment. *R. Lewis*

FRANKENHOUSE Pre-fabricated house. *R. Stephens*

GRAND DAME 1) Large, stately home. 2) Multi-family housing with the façade of a large, stately home. *R. Pflugrath AICP*

GRISWOLDIAN A house that is overly decorated with Christmas lights, etc. *J. Gloor*

HICE Plural of house. *PseudoDictionary*

HOFFICE A building that doubles as a house and office. *SlangSite*

HOME ON THE RANGE House surrounded by large expanses of open space. (cowboy) *R. Adams* [See "range"]

HUTCH 1) A hut or hovel used as a shelter by a person. 2) A house for rabbits. *Real Estate Dictionary*

KENNEL Substandard house; a dog. *P. Dickson*

LIBKEN Old slang for house or lodging. *Anon.*

MESSUAGE A house together with its adjacent buildings and surrounding land. H.F. Byrne

MICKEY MOUSE HOUSE A house with questionable design features. *R. Stephens*

MOBILE HOME MODERNE [See "factory-built home"]

MONSTER HOUSE [See "mansionization"]

OLDE WORLDE (pronounced Oldie Worldie) Cute English cottage-type dwelling, with a thatched roof, beams so low you regularly knock yourself silly, no mod cons [modern conveniences] or other facilities, preferably with an authentic outhouse. *E. Poventud*

OUTHOUSE [See "outhouse"]

PAINTED LADY [See "architectural style"]

PATIO HOUSE A detached, single-family unit typically situated on a reduced-size lot that orients outdoor activity within rear or side yard patio areas for better use of the site for outdoor living space. *CPR*

PIÑATA A home painted with gaudy colors. *K. Bradfield*

PRODUCTION HOUSES Tract houses. *W. Lutz*

RANCHBURGER A one-story generic southwestern tract house. *K. Moloney*

REPO CABIN Any house or structure that is barely inhabitable and not worth paying the mortgage or rent, better to wait and let it be repossessed. *J. Alex*

ROBIN HOOD HOUSE One with a little john. *Real Estate Humor*

SAUSAGE HOME House built on A zero lot line with only one or no sideyards at all. *B. Inman*

SINGLE FAMILY HOME A home that contains only unmarried people. *R. Reitzel*

SNOUT HOUSE A house with the garage thrust to the front of the main body of the building. Snout houses have very negative effect on the pedestrian continuity as front-loaded garages cannot express potentially interesting human activity as might a window, door or porch. The term alludes to the proboscis-like extrusion capped by the pair of garage openings as nostrils. This flaw, which is endemic to narrow-frontage housing within conventional suburban development, can be overcome only by the provision of alleys or back lanes for rear-loaded garages. Practice provides rear-loaded garages for narrow lots, although the pedestrian performance of all buildings benefits from rear access parking. *Parole*

STARTER HOME A small house. *R. Holder*

TRACT HOUSES 1) Suburban domiciles built in mass quantities along virtually identical lines, for middle-class families who lead virtually identical lives. Formerly produced at low cost; always produced at the expense of the landscape. *R. Bayan* 2) Production houses. *W. Lutz*

VERDICUUM House. *Pseudodictionary*

HouseTRAP [See "TRAP"]

housing
Architect: Statement
Building & Safety: Structure

Developer: Product
Environmentalist: Habitation
Foreign: Settlement
Homeless: Shelter
Legal: Domicile
Military: Vertical Development [See "berm"]
Planner: D.U. [See "D.U."]
Realtor: Market
Common: Home
R. Stephens

housing shortage Ugly rumor circulated by people who have no place to live. *H. Morgan*

housitosis Bad house odors. (halitosis) *Anon.* [See "sick building"]

human scale Less than 400 feet tall. *Glass Steel and Stone*

hundred percent location An appraisal term referring either to land of the highest value in an area, or land best suited to a specific use. *Real Estate Dictionary*

hyperlocal Tailored to a specific and often very small geographic area. *C. Trueheart*

hypermarket A large store on supermarket lines, but at least 5,000 square meters in area serving a population of at least 50,000. (British) *P. Tutt* [See "supermarket"]

hypertouristification Grossly excessive mass tourism. *J. Train*

hysteric preservation The preservation of historically insignificant structures and neighborhoods. *E.M. Vargas* [See "historic preservation"]

I

"I came on the bus" Effect At any public hearing, the number of different opinions expressed by the public decreases in direct proportion to the number of persons speaking. When tour buses are used to ferry angry citizens to a public hearing, the number of opinions expressed usually drops to zero. *E. Norris AICP*

identity points Thematic entry statements. *Anon.* [See "designer babble" and "memory points"]

ideological supervision Censorship. *R. Holder*

ideopolis [See "opolis"]

IGMFY "I've Got Mine, F(orget) You" *R. Galanter*

imageability The 5 elements of city imagery: paths, edges, nodes, districts, and landmarks. *K. Lynch*

imagineer, imagineering From General Electric or Disney. Imaginative construction or progression. Used primarily by marketing and sales people to describe some "leap of faith" taken by someone with regards to a project. Word is a fusion of "imagine" and "engineer(ing)." *PseudoDictionary*

impact fee The increasingly popular method by which governments assign to developers the social costs brought about by their building. The developers are made to pay for some of the new roads, sewers, water taps, and the like that have tradition- ally been provided by the taxpayers, but that would not be required were it not for the development. This has a fairness benefit in that it does not assign to existing residents the costs of providing new services to future residents. But to the extent that growth is less subsidized, it drives up the cost, which contributes to issues of affordability. *J. Garreau*

Imperial system of measurement The bizarre system of measurement using such arcane units as chains, feet, yards, furlongs, miles, sections, etc. A township, for example, is based on 19th century surveying with horses and mules. We have two measurements for a mile: 5,280 feet over land; 6,076 feet over water (nautical mile). The mile is also divided into furlongs, chains, rods, etc. most of which are a mystery to the average citizen. While the rest of the world has moved forward with the logical 'metric system,' the U.S. continues to use such bizarre units as gallons, acre-feet, cubic yards, knots, etc. *R. Stephens* [See "MILF" and "sports analogies"]

improvements Generally, buildings, but may include any permanent structure or other development, such as a street, utilities, etc. *First American Title Co.*[See "betterments"]

in the field Out of the office for a longer period than "at a meeting." The field is hypothetically the "real world" where programs are implemented. *D.E. Miller*

incongestion (congestions, indigestion) Excessive accumulation of automobiles in the community, the functions of which are thereby disordered. Also, 'dysautopsy.' *R. Stephens*

incorporeal realty The intangible elements of property and the nonmaterial rights that go with property, such as right of way or air rights. *D.E. Miller*

industrial castles Industrial development with fence-gate-guard-pass combinations, moat-like expansive buffers, and large structures perched on dramatic pen sites. *G. Clay*

industry lite Less filling than heavy industry; more taste than light industry. Examples include hi-tech and artisan industries. *R. Stephens*

inferior desecrator Interior designer. Example: A lot of homes have been spoiled by inferior desecrators. *F.L. Wright*

infrastruction The art of constructing infrastructure. *C. Guzkowski*

infrastructure 1) The structure within an infra. 2) The structure outside the infra. 3) A building with built-in infras. *P. Dickson* 4) A modern piece of cant, of no discernibly useful meaning, much employed by jargonizing social scientists. *P. Bowler* 5) The underwear of the city. Nobody wants to see it, they just want it to function properly in the background. *D. Slater* [See "outfrastructure"]

initial feasibility study An analysis of a specific project or program to determine if it can be successfully carried out. The acronym for this study is, appropriately, 'IFS.' *R. Stephens*

ink-slinger Drafter. *B. Pollack*

Inner City 1) Where the outsiders live. A black ring on the urban dartboard, sandwiched between the white downtown bull's-eye and the equally white outer ring of suburbs. Anyone who lands there automatically forfeits all his points. *R. Bayan* 2) Polite language for ghetto; where whites or landed Asians live in a city, it's called Uptown or Downtown, whichever is furthest from the inner-city. *DDX* [See "doughnut effect"]

inner-city nittygritty The clichéd cinematic atmosphere of noir films or Stephen Bochco's TV cop series 'Hill Street Blues' and 'NYPD Blue.' *J. Parker*

Ins and Outs [See "architectural ornamentation"]

insanitary landfill Any packed stadium. *R. Stephens*

Institutions
ACORN ACADEMY An institution for the mentally ill. R. Holder
BONE FACTORY Hospital
CAMP CUPCAKE Federal prison camp for women. Example: Things aren't so bad at 'Camp Cupcake' after all. Just ask Martha Stewart. *C. Amter*
CLUB FED Minimum security prison. *Anon.*
COP SHOP Police station. *J. Green*
CUCKOO'S NEST Mental hospital.
DEEP FREEZE A prison. *R. Holder*
ELEEMOSYNARY INSTITUTION Any building or group of buildings devoted to and supported by charity. *Gunee, IL* [See "eleemosynary"]
EVENTIDE HOME An institution for geriatrics. *R. Holder*
FAT FARM Obesity Clinic.
FRISBEE   Flatulent   Reactive   Institutions   Sensing   Belligerent   Ecological

Environmentalists. *M. Roos AICP*
FUNNY FARM Mental hospital
GIGGLE FARM/FACTORY Mental hospital
GOD BOX Church. *J. Green*
GOD'S WAITING ROOM A retirement institution for geriatrics. *R. Holder*
GOLGOTHA Meeting place of the heads of universities, colleges or halls. *Anon.*
GYM State penitentiary.
LOONY BIN Mental hospital
MEGACHURCH Church organizations that broadcast worship services on radio and television, reaching hundreds of thousands of listeners and viewers. *K. Watts*
NUTHOUSE Mental hospital
RURAL SLAMMER Inner-city African-American and Latino escape to the country—remote prisons. *D. Hayden*
Probert Encyclopaedia
UNI University. *J. Green*
WELLNESS CENTER Hospital. *W. Lutz*

institutional memory The oldest planner in the department who remembers historic practice, archaic policy, mythic variances, and so on. *R. Stephens*

insultant Consultant. *M. Roos AICP*

Interstate Highways An impressive asphalt circulatory system that enables a traveler to drive swiftly from Seattle to Miami without encountering a single landmark worth stopping for. *R. Bayan* [See "freeway" and "facilities"]

Inverse Appreciation, Law of The less there is between you and the environment, the more you appreciate the environment. *Anon.*

Inverse Planning Law Ruralize the city; urbanize the country. *D. Bartlett*

Iron-Plan Triathlon
1)   General Plan Amendment Drawn-and-Quartered Cycle
2)   Zone Change Sink or Swim
3)   Design Review Runaround
R. Stephens

isoscrat A contour on a map illustrating a line of constant density of muscrats. (Canadian) *T. White*

Issue Attention Cycle In the cycle, the imagination and energy of public leaders progress from alarmed discovery of a problem, to euphoric mobilization of resources and a search for solutions, to institutionalization of responses. Then the hard realities of expensive answers and slow progress come home to roost, causing a hasty retreat and a wholesale shift of attention to the newest hot issue to be fueled by yet another alarmed discovery. *J. Catterall*

Italianalienate [See "architectural style"]

ITC Information Technology and Communications. (European) *M. Schrenk*

ITNC In The Next County. *R. Mamaghani*

J

James Gang Firm of incompetent or roguish builders. (British) *Probert Encyclopaedia*

Jedi Knight A laser pointer swordsman. (Star Wars) *R. Stephens*

Jello Plan A plan that has not quite gelled. *W. Densmore*

juice A powerful pressure group or lobby. *Anon.*

jobs/housing balance The distribution of employment relative to the distribution of workers within a given geographic area. A geographic area is considered balanced when these distributions are approximately equal, and when available housing choices complement the earning potential of available jobs. When achieved, jobs-housing balance results in an adequate supply of housing (and therefore workers) being located within a reasonable distance of compatible employment opportunities. *WRCOG*

Joe/John
JOE BLOGGS Average or typical man. (British)
JOE BLOW Average or ordinary man.
JOE BROWN Rhyming slag for a town. (British)
JOE PLANNER Typical planner
JOE PUBLIC General public.
JOE SHMO Average or typical man.
JOE SIXPACK Average or typical man.
JOHN DOE Unidentified male
JOHN FARMER Imaginary ordinary farmer
JOHN Q CITIZEN Average man-in-the-street
[The feminine version is 'Jill'] *Probert Encyclopaedia*

joint adventure A combining by two or more persons of their property, skill, efforts, etc., for a specific business purpose. Single purpose partnerships are now most commonly used and are based on the same idea of the single purpose business venture. *Real Estate Dictionary*

Jolly Green Giant 'The Practice of Local Planning' by ICMA. *Anon.*

journey to work Commute. *J. Stephens*

juggernaut Large commercial vehicles at present maximum 32.5 tons, but on the Continent (Europe) up to 30 tons. (British) *P. Tutt*

jungle Previous term for a dangerous natural environment which has been replaced with the greenwash term "rain forest". "Jungle" now refers to the more dangerous urban environment [i.e. asphalt jungle]. Also related to the use of "zoo" to describe urban chaos. *R. Stephens* [See "badlands," "green" and "zoo"]

junior executive studio Tiny [500-square-foot] condo. *R. Ryon* [See "condominia"]

K

Keeper of the Keys The individual in an organization who controls critical functions, but who may not have recognizable authority or position title.

kennel [See "house"]

Kevlar coating [See "bullet-proof"]

key lot [See "lot"]

kickback Illegal rebate. *Real Estate Dictionary*

killer litter Garbage tossed from a high-rise building. *K. Whiting*

kiosk An open pavilion such as a bandstand or newsstand. Used to describe the structures in the open areas of malls that sell specialty items. *Real Estate Dictionary* 2) Street furniture column for public announcements. *R. Stephens*

Kiss & Ride When a loved one drops you at the transit station. *P. Calthorpe*

kit of parts A limited number of design elements repeated endlessly throughout a development in the hope that such recapitulation will give the project an identity. *J. Garreau*

Kobayashi Maru Scenario The scenario where the project is destined to be denied by the Planning Commission, but designed to be approved by City Council on appeal. The Planning Commission hearing is a 'test of character.' (Star Trek) *R. Stephens* [See "near death experience"]

Kommissar Commissioner. (German) Example: 'Alles klar, Herr Kommissar?' *R. Stephens*

L

LAFCO Local Agency Formation COmmission. Public agency which determines special district boundaries, sphere of influence boundaries, and annexations. "LAFCO cuts the pie." The story of towns competing for intervening land is *A Sale of Two Cities*. *E.M. Vargas*

lake
Engineering: retention basin
Fish & Wildlife: wetlands
Landscaping: water feature
Marketing: aquatic amenity
Recreation: swimming facility
British: pawnee
Common: pond
R. Stephens

La-la land A place where the Tooth Fairy and Dracula have tea parties and people visit quite often when extrenely bored. Other residents include the Easter Bunny, Bigfoot, and a bowl of munchkins. Not enough munchkins for a symphony, but enough for a big band sound from the 1930s and 1940s. *S. McCool*

land bank An accumulation of land held for future use. *Real Estate Dictionary*

land bank robbery Inverse condemnation. *R. Stephens* [See "land donor"]

land donor Synonymous with 'land owner.' A property owner who must often relinquish land through dedications, exactions, easements, etc. in order to develop the remainder. Also appropriate for someone subject to inverse condemnation and trespassing. *J. Stephens* [See "claim jumper" and "trespass"]

land value law The value of any parcel of land is determined by three factors. The first is location. The second is location. And the third is location. *J. Clapp*

land yacht An extremely large car especially from the 70s. *J. M.*

landlocked [See "-lock"]

landromat Real estate office. *E.M. Vargas*

landscraper Landscape architect. *R. Esteban*

landsman 1) One who lives and works on land. 2) Friend. *J. Green*

Large Lot Law Size matters. *R. Masyczek* [See "laws"]

Laser Pointer Parkinson's A disorder of the presentation characterized by tremor and impaired laser pointer coordination. *R. Stephens*

laserium [See "public hearing/meeting']

The Late Great Outdoors Disappearing open space. *E.M. Vargas*

latté litigation Legal actions regarding coffee stores. *ihatestarbucks.com*

Lavelle Amendment Creatively written findings for approval of a desired, but questionable, variance. *M. Multari*

laws [See individual listing and "rules"]
BALZER'S LAW
BRUCE-BRIGG'S LAW OF TRAFFIC
FIRST LAW OF ECOLOGY
FIRST LAW OF PROPERTY
FIRST LAW OF PUBLIC LAND
FIRST LAW OF TINKERING
INVERSE PLANNING LAW
LAND VALUE LAW
LARGE LOT LAW
LAW OF ROAD CONSTRUCTION
LAW OF INVERSE APPRECIATION
LAW OF NATIONS
McCLAUGHRY'S IRON LAW OF ZONING
NATURAL LAWS OF PUBLIC HEARINGS [See "Public Hearings, Natural Laws of"]
PARKINSON'S FIFTH LAW
PUBLIC HEARINGS, NATURAL LAWS OF
SPECIES AREA LAW
STEPHENS' LAW OF RIGHT OF WAY [See "right of way"]
WOLF'S PLANNING LAW
WOOD'S LAW

Law of Nations In an underdeveloped country, don't drink the water; in a developed country, don't breathe the air. *Anon.* [See "developmenr" and "laws"]

lawn ornaments Outdoor sculpture for the artistically innocent, who take pleasure in the contrasting tonalities of flamingo and grass, or in the robust texture of a painted plaster jockey with a ring through its nose. *R. Bayan*   [See "architectural ornamentation" and "yard garbage"]

lawyer 1) People who go in after the auditors and strip the bodies. [See "auditor"] 2) Legal accomplice. *W. Ballbach* 3) One skilled in the circumvention of the law. *A. Bierce* [See "terms of venery"]

lawyer fodder Planning issue which hasn't been tested. *R. Schonholtz*

lawyer-to-lawyer [rule of thumb] Whenever one side brings a lawyer, the other must, too. Otherwise it's like having a knife at a gunfight. *A. Davies*

lay of the land 1) General environment. (cowboy) *R. Adams* 2) Skillful practitioner of the oldest profession. *Anon.* [See "mottos"]

Layer-Cake Model Biological and geological factor map overlays [McHargian]. *F. Steiner*

lead agency The public agency which has the principal responsibility for carrying out a project [sometimes on a stretcher]. *R. Stephens*

lead screening The bullet-proof dais partition for public officials to duck behind in the event an angry citizen chooses to exercise their right to fire arms. Example: "The new city council chambers have Kevlar panels behind the dais partition instead of steel." *R. Stephens*

leap-frogging Land development that skips close-in space for outlying areas; the purpose is to develop less costly land. *Kenneth Leventhal & Company* [Often the municipality will (stand) erect in the developer's mid-leap with predictable conse-quences.]

Lebensraum   Unincorporated area to be annexed. From the Nazi term for 'living space'—conquered territory. (German). *A. Davies* [See "annexoria nervosa," "fear of influence" and "protectorate"]

leeches   Journalists, politicians, attorneys, regulators, government planners, environmental lobbyists, bureaucrats, and the perpetrators of all other sniveling, caviling occupations seen as producing nothing of value, at great expense to those who do, i.e. the developers, who coined the word. *J. Garreau*

less filling; more taste   Residential development with smaller units, but more amenities. *R. Stephens*

less is more   1) The designer ran out of ideas. *Glass Steel and Stone*   2) More time. More money. More headache. *Anon.*

Let the games begin   Ancient Roman expression to open the public meeting between the lions and the slaves. *R. Stephens* [See "public hearing/meeting"]

Let's Make a Deal Phenomenon   Sequence of events whereby commuters arriving in their street distinguish their home by pressing the garage door opener and entering the garage door that opens. *UCLA* [See "public hearing"]

Level of Service 'F' (LOS F)   The point at which a street becomes a parking lot. The traffic planner's 'F' word. The worst conceivable traffic congestion is LOS FU. *R. Stephens*

Lichtenberg's Insight [See "zone/zoning"]

lifestyle enclaves Named by sociologist Robert Bellah. He believes that we are replacing traditional communities, which are characterized by a true population diversity, with clusters of people who are linked by shared values and habits, and who seek the security of sameness. *F. Popcorn*

lightbulbs How many bureaucrats does it take to change a lightbulb? Two. One to assure you everything is fine; the other to screw the lightbulb into the faucet. [See "bureaucrat"]

Lilliput Syndrome The "magic" of miniature models. Small things are considered "cute" and this is never truer than with models of projects that have miniature people, cars and trees. This affinity for "neotenic" (youthful) things has a different psychological reaction than the full-size, real world projects. *R. Stephens* [See "animals, miniature"]

liquidated damages A penalty for failing to achieve the impossible. *Nevada Nut & Bolt, Inc.*

liquor license limit [rule of thumb] No more than three liquor licenses within a 1-mile radius. Not within 1,000 feet of a church or school. *K. Gonzales*

litter on a stick [See "signage"]

local identity corrosion The infusion of chain stores that do not reflect the character of a neighborhood. *Prince Charles*

-lock Inability to move; paralysis; a jam. *D. Barnhart*

AQUALOCK [of a harbor]

BOATLOCK [of, surprisingly, boats]

CABLOCK [of taxi traffic]

GREENLOCK Traffic gridlock common at national forests and parks especially during the summer tourist season. *S. Lerner*

GRIDLOCK 1) Freeway parking. *R. Stephens* 2) Originally referred to third-world traffic congestion created by pervasive non-enforcement of traffic laws. Today sometimes used to refer to a legal impasse, which prevents clearcutting in many forests. Gridlock is usually unmistakable evidence that activists have been successful in thwarting the devious plans of large corporations. So Gridlock is a badge of honor and a measure of effectiveness. *J. Britell*

GRIDLUCK One's good fortune in finding a viable alternate route around a traffic mess. *N. Israel*

LANDLOCK Property that has no access to a public road. *Kenneth Leventhal & Company*

PEDLOCK [of pedestrians]

SUPERGRIDLOCK A gigantic traffic jam extending over many miles, especially beyond the limits of a single city. *The New York Times*

WINGLOCK [of aircraft] *K. Steele*

looking at houses [rule of thumb] In house building, the lighter the framing, the more recent the construction. *G Koos* [See "houses"]

loops and lollipops Street pattern of loop connections and cul-de-sacs. *J.M. Fernandez AICP* [See "dead worm syndrome" and "spaghetti bowl"]

Los Angelization Uncontrolled growth of a city's population and traffic congestion, crime, pollution, and other such socio-economic problems. *K. Watts* [See "Californication"]

lost in translation When public officials misunderstand the case and/or motion and vote the opposite of what they intended. *R. Stephens*

lot A subdivision of land; a building site; the debris- and bottle-infested area that occupies space before it becomes a ranchero or high-rise. *D.E. Miller*
BACK/LOWER FORTY Extremely large cul-de-sac lot. *R. Stephens*
BEAUTY-SPOT Lot with an exceptional location. *R. Stephens*
BLANK What residential developers call land. A blank is a lot on which a house can be built. As in blank slate. But more important, it is a basic conceptual unit. Land is not a meaningful commodity to a residential builder until it has been reduced to Blanks by a process that includes taking the entire amount of land available, subtracting that on which homes cannot be built (because of provisions for parks, floodplains, roads, shopping centers, and the like), and dividing the remainder by the total number of homes the developer can get zoning for. *J. Garreau*
BROKEN WINDOW LOT Golf course frontage subject to errant golf balls. *A. Davies*
CAMELOT Large lot with 'starter castle.' *R. Stephens* [See "Camelot"]
CLOT Single obstructive lot. *R. Stephens*
COLUMN LOTS Small lots for the placement of columns to support a structure, such as a billboard or other structure which has its largest parts not touching the ground. *Real Estate Dictionary*
DOUBLE FRONTAGE/LOADED LOT Streets on both front and back. *R. Stephens*
FLAG LOT A lot not fronting on or abutting a public road and where access to the public road is by a narrow, private right-of-way. In some jurisdictions, a "red flag" lot. *A. Davies*

HAMLET LOT A small residential lot located in a contiguous group, with adjacent and fronting lots oriented toward each other in some ordered geometric way--as on a street, a green or a paved square—and forming a distinct boundary with the surrounding countryside. *Loudon County, VA*

HOMESITE User-friendly term for "lot". *R. Stephens*

KEY LOT Lot that has added value because of its strategic location. *Kenneth Leventhal & Company*

LETTERED LOT Subdivision lot not for residential development (a numbered lot). *A. Davies*

LOT SAMMICH Double frontage lot. *R. Stephens*

MANUFACTURED LOT A lot upon which construction of a building may begin. Having all off-site improvements and approvals of government agencies. *Real Estate Dictionary*

MIRROR LOT A proposed lot that is similar in appearance to an existing lot. The mirror lot is designed to be compatible to existing development. *R. Stephens*

ORPHAN LOT In a subdivision, a plot of land marked as a housing lot, but considered unbuildable because of terrain or environmental constraints. *K. Drohan*

OUTLOT A lot remnant or parcel of land left over after platting, which is intended as open space or other use, for which no building permit shall be issued. *Buffalo, MN*

PANHANDLE LOT Same as "flag lot." *A. Davies*

PARKING LOT Subdivision for cars. *R. Stephens*

PIPESTEM LOT A "panhandle" or "flag"-shaped lot with its widest point set back from the road at the rear of another lot (called the pipe), and having a thin strip of land connecting to the road to provide legal access and frontage (called the stem). *Blacksburg, VA*

PONDEROSA, THE The 'alpha' lot in a subdivision. Often the lot designed for the owner or developer. *R. Stephens*

PORK CHOP LOT An interior lot requiring a long driveway to reach the main part of the property. *D. Hayden*

POSTAGE STAMP LOT Very small lot. This is a relative term— what is today called an "estate" would have been considered a postage stamp lot years ago. *R. Stephens* [See "estate" and "residential scale"]

REGULAR LOT One shaped like a square or a triangle, with front and back edges of equal lengths. *D.E. Miller*

SHOEBOX LOT A very small, walled lot resembling a shoe box. *M. Madden*

THROUGH LOT Double frontage lot. *H. Moskowitz*

TIME SLOT Time share lot. *Anon.*

TOT LOT Small lot devoted to a playground. *Anon.*

WIDE BODY LOT Wide but shallow building lots that save land and permit builders to pack more homes onto smaller sites. *B. Inman*

YACHT LOT Boat slip. *R. Stephens*

ZIPPER LOT A version of the wide-and-shallow lot with the garage on the side, which lines up with the backyard of another lot in the rear. *B. Inman* [See "house," "residential scale," and "sports analogies"]

GROUCHO: Do you know what a lot is?

CHICO: Yeah, too much.

GROUCHO: I don't mean a whole lot. Just a little lot with nothing on it.

CHICO: Any time you gotta too much, you gotta whole lot. Look, I'll explain it to you. Some time you no gotta much; sometimes you gotta whole lot. You know that it's a lot. Somebody else maybe thinka it's too much; it's a whole lot, too. Now, a whole lot is too much; too much is a whole lot; same thing. *Cocoanuts* [See "house"]

Lot Line Adjustment [LaLA] A minor change in a lot line between two parcels. Creative lot line adjustments [lala's] attempt to create <u>more</u> lots and land.

lot sammich [See "lot"]

lotting study Map showing how a property may be subdivided. *R. Stephens*

lottoplan Plan with a one in a million chance of getting built. *R. Stephens*

low bidder A consultant who is wondering what he left out. *Nevada Nut & Bolt, Inc.*

low maintenance [See "real estate sales glossary"]

Lubbock [See "rural country"]

LULU Locally unacceptable land use. *F. Popper* [See "Nimbyism" and "ZOTs"]

luminaires Designer-babble for "lights." *R. Stephens* [See "designer-babble"]

LUST Leaking underground storage tank.

M

machi zukuri City-making. (Japanese) *Y. Kumata*

MAD [See "density game"]

magic of miniaturization [See "Lilliput Syndrome"]

Magic Phrase, The Simple expression for unlocking or translating an urban situation to its inhabitants or its visitors. Also, 'Golden Key.' *G. Clay*

magnet store   The largest retail establishment in a shopping center that draws customers and thereby generates business for the remaining stores in the center.   *H. Moskowitz*

MAH Multifamily Affordable Housing.   *Real Estate Dictionary*

main drag Primary thoroughfare.   *K. Watts*

Main Street   A broad and imposing thoroughfare that generally runs through a district of empty storefronts. *R. Bayan*

mall parkers [See "parkers, mall"]

mall, vestigal A number of speciality shops at the entrance to a hypermarket.   *P. Tutt* [See "hypermarket"]

mallburbia The business community that has developed in the vicinity of a mall.   *D. McKenney* [See "suburbia" and "zoo"]

mallmanac Mall kiosk.   *B. Dellman* [See "kiosk"]

man cave An area of a house, such as a basement, workshop, or garage, where a man can be alone with his power tools and projects. *M. Hiestand* [See "cul-de-sac caves"]

mandamus 1) Latin for *we command*. A writ issued by a superior court ordering an inferior court, corporation, or individual, to do or refrain from doing specific acts. The main importance to real estate is that it is a writ commanding a governmental body to do something, such as issue a building permit. *Real Estate Dictionary*

mansionization 1) Conversion of older small homes on small lots to new, large homes with maximum coverage. "Making mansions out of infills." *R. Stephens*
BIG HAIR HOUSE A house that has a garish style and that is overly large compared to its lot size and to the surrounding houses. *S. Wood*
HOUSE ON STEROIDS *B. Inman*
McMANSION A large, opulent house, especially a new house that has a size and style that doesn't fit in with the surrounding houses. *S. Kaplan*
MONSTER HOUSE *M. Best*
SINGLE FAMILY MINI-CASTLE *G. Harbeck*
STARTER CASTLE A large house built on a lot so small there's no room for the moat. Generally resented by the neighbors for its ostentatious display of affluence -- and frequently bad taste. *M. Matthews*
TEARDOWN Home bought to be replaced by a larger one. *J. Adler*
TRACT MANSION The ultimate subdivision house. A residence of extraordinary size [four thousand square feet and up] and expense [approaching a million dollars or more] built amid homes that are very similar, if not identical. Tract mansions are distinct from estates in that they are located on relatively tiny plots of land, sometimes as little as a sixth of an acre. *J. Garreau*

manufactured home [See "factory-built home"]

mapalicious Aesthetic appearance on a map. Example: "The shape of Italy sure is mapalicious." *Kris*

mapster Cartographer, planner. *R. Stephens*

marble orchard Graveyard. *Probert Eneyclopaedia*

marginal land 1) Any income producing land which barely covers expenses. 2) Land which is clearly not the best for an intended purpose, but may be adequate. *Real Estate Dictionary*

market Economic activity in which buyers and sellers come together and the forces of supply and demand affect prices; a fuzzy compulsive entity often spoken of as "The Market" to explain why good planning design must give way to such factors as real estate deals, bank financing concerns, redevelopment schemes, etc. *P. Clark*

marketecture The formulaic architecture of superstores. *R. Stephens*

married to a plan Unwillingness to deviate from an original plan. *A. Davies* "Married to the plan and divorced from reason." Planimony.

mass transit For others, not me. *R. Castillo*

massage the plan Cut back and simplify a design. *K. Moloney*

matrix evaluation A table full of rough numbers designed to sum up to a predetermined outcome. *J. Hingtgen* [See "number crunching"]

Mayberry Mentality New urbanist developments. *R. Kroloff* [See "neotraditionalism"]

MBWA Management By Walking Around. *W. H. Claire III, AICP*

McAlpine's Fusiliers Building laborers. (British) *Probert Encyclopaedia*

MCIP My Career Is Painful. (Member, Canadian Institute of Planners) *J. Hay MCIP* [See "AICP" and "MRTPI"]

mcguffin Movie term, invented by Hitchcock, to refer to any interchangeable object—diamonds, secret plans, computer disk, rare animal etc.—that is the focus of the action in the plot, but which has no significance to the plot itself. Example: "The project had numerous significant issues, but the Council focused on the mcguffin of backyard pools." *A. Leslie* [See "delicate detail" and "devilish detail"]

McClaughry's Iron Law of Zoning When it's not needed, zoning works fine; when it is essential, it always breaks down. [See "zone/zoning"]

McMansion [See "house" and "mansionization"]

McPlace Standardized "sense of place". *R. E. Knack* [See "anyplace syndrome" and "nullibiety"]

meetingcide [See "public hearing/meeting"]

mega-city [See "opolis" and "city"]

megalopolis [See "opolis"]

megastructure Structure or a unified complex that contains at least one million square feet. *Kenneth Leventhal & Company*

megazoo [See "zoo"]

MEGO Mine Eyes Glaze Over. Used humorously, a *mego* is an event, performance, or piece of writing or art that produces dazed boredom in the observer. Also used adjectivally as in "the mego factor." *H. Lemay* [See "Perelman's Point"]

Meisterplanner An artistic or epic planner. *M. Schrenk*

memo pause Cessation in the flow of memos. *L.V. Eaton*

memory point An element of a development meant to be regarded as so spectacular as to stick in the client's mind long after he or she has gotten home that night. *J. Garreau* [See "delicate detail," "devilish detail," and "Moby's Dick"]

ménage abbatoir Design Review Board threesome butchery. *E.M. Vargas*

messuage [See "house"]

meteor strip The patch of land between lanes on the highway. *Pseudodictionary*

metes and bounds Description of land by boundary lines, with their terminal points and angles. Originally metes referred to distance, bounds to direction; modernly, the words have no individual meaning of practical significance. *Real Estate Dictionary* [See "Imperial system of measurement"]

metropolis [See "opolis"]

metrowoods A wooded park area in the midst of a city. *P. Edic* [See "ambassadors of the forest in the town"]

MFR Memorandum For Record; a written memo recalling what went on at a given meeting. *P. Dickson* 2) In simpler times, *minutes*. [see "paper trail"]

microbrewery [See "brew pub"]

microrelief Minor surface changes, such as channels, dunes, or low hummocks, rather than hills or mountains. *First American Title Company*

Midnight Meeting Effect [rule of thumb] Describes the fact that, at any public hearing, the amount of public testimony on an item increases in direct proportion to its triviality. *E. Norris AICP* [See "public hearing"]

MIGA Make It Go Away. *Anon.*

mileway The time required to walk one mile. [About 12-15 minutes on level ground] *H.F. Byrne*

MILF Measured In Linear Feet. Derogatory expressions for Euclidean zoning code parameters. *E.M. Vargas* [See "Imperial system of measurement"]

milk a project To unnecessarily extend work on a project for additional payment or other benefit. *D. Parton*

MILTFPFOS Make It Like The F****** Plans For Once, Stupid! *M. Roos AICP*

mini-street A bike trail that is so long it resembles a street. *Nick*

mining trees Logging. *J. Kunstler*

mischief alley Any place where unexpectedly funny things can happen. *S. Beyer*

mitigation measures Minor additions to a project to allow it to narrowly pass the environmental review. *J. Hingtgen*

mixed use The kitchen in every home. *R. Castillo*

mixed use development (MUD/MXD) [rule of thumb] Three or more revenue producing land uses. *ULI*

Moby's Dick The feature of a project that a decision-maker obsesses on with little or no consideration for any other aspect. *E.M. Vargas* [See "delicate detail" and "devilish detail"]

model home An idealized version of what a home in a development or unit in a condominium will look like after it has been bought and put into shape. Model homes or model units are real estate sales aids, meant to entice potential buyers with the possibilities of the property being sold. *D.E. Miller*

moditerranean [See "architectural style"]

modular home [See "factory-built home"]

mom and pop operation [Mop Op] Term for small family business, investors, applicants... Expression implies naïveté, inexperience, and limited resources— American Gothic. *Anon.*

mom and pop store Corner shops. *J. Green*

mommy traffic The afternoon weekday, non-peek hour shopping demographic. (Also, 'soccer-mom traffic') *T. Austin*

Monet, a Project that looks good at first glance, but not after closer examination. *Anon.*

monolithic sidewalk Engineering term for a sidewalk adjacent the curb. A sidewalk not adjacent the curb: 'nonolithic sidewalk.' *R. Stephens*

monster house [See "house" and "mansionization"]

monster-planned community A master-planned community of inordinate size. *R. Stephens* [See "MPC"]

monumentenmoe [See "sightsee-sick"]

moon, to To situate a building so that its back side is presented to another building in a distasteful fashion. *J. Garreau*

MOOT Move Out Of Town. Reduction of troop concentrations in cities. *D. Hauptman*

moratorium [or Interim Control Ordinance] A prohibition on construction usually enacted to prevent a development which otherwise could have been built By Right. After it is enacted, it becomes the basis for convincing the developer to voluntarily change his project. *D. Ring* Also, 'nomorium.'

motel A convenient roadside inn that shelters tired travelers and libidinous locals. *R. Bayan*

mottos 1) "Planners know the right zones." *R. Stephens* 2) "We the unwilling, led by the unknowing, are so used to doing so much with so little that we now believe we can do anything with nothing." [Ranger's Rule] *J. Freiman* 3) "Planners have designs." *refrigerator magnet* 4) "Planning without action is futile; action without planning is fatal." *F. Sherkow* 5) Planners know the lay of the land and where to find her/him. *Anon.* 6) "Plan or perish." *H.W. Struben* 7) Planners do it with permission. (British) *N. O'Byrne* 8) We have lots to be thankful for. *Real Estate Humor* 9) Be regionable. *R. Esteban*

MPC Master-Planned Camelot. (master-planned community) *R. Stephens* [See "Camelot"]

MRTPI Maximum Response Time for Permission Issuance (Member of the Royal Town Planning Institute) [See "AICP" and "MCIP"]

MSCT Mall Standard Closing Time: 9:00 p.m. *H. Shearer*

MTV More Trees and Vines. [See "MVP"]

multidimensional gaming with an entertainment complex Casino *W. Lutz*

multidisciplinary services A special kind of sadomasochism. *J. Marquez*

multi-modal transportation Walking to your car. *R. Stephens*

multi-pass The amenities, concessions, designs, etc. required for multi-family affordable housing approvals. (Fifth Element) *R. Stephens*

municrat A municipal bureaucrat. *S. Newman*

MVP More Vines, Please. Efforts to screen ugly architecture with landscaping. 'Vines' may be replaced with eucalyptus, ivy, etc. *M. Roos. AICP* [See "MTV"]

MXD [See "mixed use development"]

N

nabe Suburban slang for 'neighborhood.' *Probert Encyclopaedia* [See "hood"]

NAP 1) Not A Part. 2) Not Acceptable Plan. 3) Non-Alert Planner. *C. Leach*

natatorium An indoor swimming pool. *H.F. Byrne*

natural resources [See "resources"]

naturalist camp Euphemism for 'nudist colony.' *A. Davies*

nature The dirt and debris on your shoes and clothing from being outside. (British)

near death experience (NDE) A 3-2 [or 4-3] public hearing vote or other close public official decision. Experiences of planners after their projects have been pronounced clinically dead, or been very close to death. Typical features of the NDE are an out-of-body-experience, life review, a tunnel experience, light, coming to a boundary (marking death), seeing former dead projects, experiencing a loving or divine presence, and making a choice (or being told) to return. Occasionally NDEs can be frightening and distressing. NDEs often have profound effects on the planner's later life. *R. Stephens* [See "count to three" and "Kobayashi Maru Scenario"]

neg dec (ND) Negative Declaration. Determination by public planning agency that a project will have no significant impact on the environment. The Neg Deck in development poker has two playing cards and 50 jokers. Also, Mitigated Negative Declaration (MND) *Anon.*

negative traffic impact Traffic jam. *J. Leach*

neighbor In the early days of our language, in the times that we call Old English, this was a compound word, made up of the two elements, *neah* and *gebur*. These separately have descended to us as "nigh" and "boor," and that is exactly what neighbor originally meant—a nearby rustic or peasant, a husbandman dwelling nearby. From the origin it would appear, therefore, that the term applies only to countryfolk and to small villages, but it was early taken into the towns and cities and applied to anyone who lived nearby. *C. Funk*

neighborhood Any collection of hitherto unacquainted individuals with physically proximate homes who find themselves suddenly united in vigorous opposition to unpalatable change, especially a rezoning, development, or highway. *J. Garreau* [See "community", "LULU", and "NIMBY"]

neighborhood serving commercial establishments Plannerese for 'stores.' *J. Leach*

neighborhood watch Neighborhood vigilante group. *G. Clay*

neighborhoodwink Take in a neighborhood by deceptive means. *R. Esteban*

neighburgerhood The area in any town where you'd find a Burger King, McDonald's, or any other fast food restaurant within close proximity of each other. *J.P. Mueller*

neoecological boundary Fence. *W. Lutz*

Neo-Taco [See "architectural style"]

Neo-Traditionalism Or how to turn the clock back to a time that never existed. *M. Kahn*
NEO-CONTEMPO PLANNING   The sequel to neo-traditional planning. *C. Brandstetter*
NEO-TRADITIONAL PLANNING Reinventing the Village. *S. Sutro* Idealized by the suburban 'Andy of Mayberry' and contrasted to the urban 'Nightmare on Elm Street.'
NEOTRAD   Short for neo-traditionalist. One who tries to embody anachronistic behaviours or appearance. Example: "Where are all these neotrads coming from; there isn't a retro shop in this town." *SlangSite*
PO-MO TRADITIONAL PLANNING Post modern planning: sprawl. *R. Stephens*
PSEUDO-TRADITIONAL PLANNING A replica of traditional planning that misses

key factors such as affordability. *R. Stephens*

RETRO-TRADITIONAL PLANNING Past traditional planning.

NEPA Non-Essential Plants and Animals. *T. Slade* [See "CEQA"]

nerdistan New suburbs and master planned communities for scientific researchers. One example is found in the Triangle Park located in North Carolina. Centennial campus is a self-defined technolopolis connected by trails and common interests to North Carolina State University in Raleigh. Centennial is a live/work campus which researchers could conceivably never leave. In addition to research facilities, the campus development includes condominiums, a magnet middle school, a hotel, a golf course and a retail town center. The campus has re-created the pleasures of home without any of its problems. For many the "hard" side of tech [science and engineering], this is a made to order environment. *J. Kotkin* [See "cyberpark," "MPC," and "opolis"]

netcafé [See "restaurant"]

NETMA Nobody Ever Tells Me Anything. *Private Planning Perspectives*

new settlements Places built especially for retired planners. *W. Wasels*

New Urbanism A community design philosophy that favors the return of a new home development with such traditional features as prominent front porches, backyard garages, multi-use buildings, and housing clustered near commercial service areas.

NGE Not Good Enough. *A. Lawler*

NIH Not Invented Here. Agency unwillingness to accept concepts, programs, etc. not originated by that agency. *S. Preston* [See "nimbyism"]

Nimbyism
BANYs Builders Against NIMBYs [Not In My Back Yard Activists]. *B. Inman*

GOAH Gedoudaheah. *Sopranos*

GOOMBA Get out of my business area. *R. Stephens*

GOOMBY Get out of my backyard. *M. Beardslee*

GUMBY Gaze upon my backyard. Opponents of residential walls and fences. *R. Stephens*

KIIMBY Keep it in my back yard. *W. Grimes*

NIABY Not in anyone's backyard. *Anon.*

NIMBY Not in my backyard. *Websters*

NIMD Not in my district. *M. Winogrond*

NIMEY Not in my election year. *M. Beardslee*

NIMFOS Not in my field of sight. *R. Stephens*

NIMFYE Not in my front yard either. *Treasure Coast Section, APA*

NIMTOO Not in my term of office. *M. Winogrond & C. Myer*

NITL Not in this lifetime. *SlangSite*

NOPE Not on planet earth. A person or attitude that opposes all real estate development or other projects that would harm the environment or reduce property values. *R. Mamaghani*

NORF No observable redeeming features. *SlangSite*

NOT "We'll have <u>None Of That</u>" Syndrome. *B Lewis*

NOTE Not over there either. *D. Rowan*

NUMBY Not under my back yard. A person who hopes or seeks to keep some dangerous or unpleasant underground feature out of his or her neighborhood. *D.*

Grann

PIITBY Put it in their back yard. *Treasure Coast Section*

QUIMBY Quit urbanizing in my backyard. *R. Stephens*

WIIFM What's in it for me? *S. Lackey AICP*

YIMBY Yes in my backyard. *Anon.*

nimbystanders (NIMBY, bystanders) Those who wait for somebody else to broach community issues: the silent majority. *S. Betts*

Nine Circles of Hell

[from Dante's *Inferno*]

Circle One: Limbo—Good projects that died in bad places.

Circle Two: Technical Torture—When legislative interpretations confront good sense.

Circle Three: Inherited Sins—Old approvals implemented today.

Circle Four: Unmet Expectations—Projects that meet standards but community tastes have changed.

Circle Five: Neighbor vs. Neighbor [I]—Conflicts between legal, conforming uses.

Circle Six: Neighbor vs. Neighbor [II]—Conflicts caused by illegal uses.

Circle Seven: More Than One Master —Interjurisdictional projects.

Circle Eight: Mobile Homes—[enough said!]. [See "factory-built home"]

Circle Nine: Potential Chaos—Ballot box planning in extremis.

M. Multari

no net loss If it holds water, it doesn't go. *H. Eng AICP*

nomorium Moratorium. *R. Stephens* [See "moratorium"]

non-comforting use (non-conforming use) A land use that was valid when brought into existence, but by subsequent development becomes no longer compatible. *R. Stephens* [See "compatible land use" and "ZOT!"]

nonolithic sidewalk [See "monolithic sidewalk"]

nonwetlands Drylands. *C. Chipping* [See "wetlands"]

NORC Naturally Occurring Retirement Community. Neighborhoods that spontaneously attract unusually large numbers of the elderly. *J. Garreau* [See "Persons of Longevity," "golden age ghettos," "raisin ranch" and "wrinkle ranch"]

notorious possession A requirement for adverse possession. Possession so open (notorious) that the owner is presumed to have notice of it and its extent. *Real Estate Dictionary*

Nouveau-Prairie Style [See "architectural style"]

NRUS Neighbors aRe US. *APA*

nullibiety State of being nowhere. *P. Bowler* [See "anyplace syndrome" and "McPlace"]

number cooking [Number Massaging] Manipulation of statistics for a specific goal. Conversion of "raw" data. *Anon.* [See "cookbook planning" and "number crunching"]

number crunching Statistical *cuisinart* processing prior to "number cooking." *Anon.* [See "bean counter" and "number cooking"]

nut, the Overhead. *Real Estate Dictionary*

O

oatmeal architecture [See "architectural style"]

oats 'n' goats A rural, western residential development with animal-keeping. *J. Stephens*

OBE Overcome By Events. *M. Beardslee* [also OTE "OverTaken by Events"] Said of a program, report, or concern that has been rendered [obsolete] by time. *P. Dickson*

oecodomic Architectural. *H.F. Byrne*

office building design [rule of thumb] A well-planned office building should be able to accommodate one person for every 225 square feet of floor space. *W. Payne*

ohnosecond That miniscule fraction of time in which you realize that you've just made a BIG mistake. *Anon.*

old-fashioned [See "real estate glossary"]

Olde Worlde [See "house"]

on-time-and-under-budget Utterly devoid of imagination. A slur used by architects. *J. Garreau*

One Hundred Percent Location A prime site; a locale thought to have all the desirable attributes for development, from image to accessibility, and none of the negatives. In practice, a phrase used to describe the geography of all development schemes for which financing is still up in the air. *J. Garreau*

one-stop shop Local government office where all aspects of development may be processed. I.e. planning, building & safety, public works, etc. *E.M. Vargas*

Ooh-Ah An unusual amenity inserted into a development specifically to elicit an animated reaction from a client. *J. Garreau*

OOSOOM Out Of Sight; Out Of Mind. A code enforcement concept. *R. Stephens*

open kimono Report or presentation revealing all the facts. "Letting it all hang out." *R. Stephens*

open space Any parcel or area of land or water essentially unimproved and set aside, dedicated, designated or reserved for public or private use of enjoyment, or for the use and enjoyment of owners and occupants of land adjoining or neighboring such open space. Open space is, coincidentally, often undevelopable. *Anon.* [See "park, natural"]

open space continuum The scale of human influence on open space starting with land that has never been touched by human hand to open space that is completely artificial. There may be some small spot in the Antarctic in the former, but more of the world is shifting—via environmental management—to the latter. *R. Stephens* [See "megazoo"]

-opolis

AEROTROPOLIS A city in which the layout, infrastructure, and economy are centered around a major airport. *Bao* [See "city, airport city"]

BOOBOPOLIS An imaginary hick town. *H.F. Byrne*

COSMOPOLITAN Having constituent elements from all over the world or from many different parts of the world.

ECUMENOPOLIS Merging of all megalopolises covering the globe with a single conurbation. *A. Toynbee*

GERITOLITAN Related to senior citizens. *R. Stephens*

IDEOPOLIS A postindustrial metropolitan area dominated by knowledge-based industries and institutions, such as universities and research hospitals. *R. Teixeira* [See "cyberpark" and "nerdistan"]

MEGALOPOLIS Modern word describing a heavily populated continuous urban area including many cities.

METROPOLIS "I never write 'metropolis' for seven cents because I can get the same price for 'city.'" *M. Twain*

MICROPOLITAN Relating to an area that has an urban center surrounded by one or more counties or regions, and that has a population between 10,000 and 50,000; relating to a small city. *J. Russell*

NECROPOLIS Cemetery.

NEOPOLITAN 1) Resident of Naples. 2) A blend of 3 flavors or styles.

PALTRIPOLITAN An insular city dweller. *H.F. Byrne*

PETOPOLIS [See "pet resort"]

PLANOPOLIS Planning board game. *R. Stephens*

POSHOPOLIS I.e. Beverly Hills *H. Shearer*

TOPOPOLITAN Limited to a certain area; opposed to *cosmopolitan*. *H.F. Byrne*

oppidan 1) Pertaining to a town. 2) A town resident. *H.F. Byrne*

oracle When a counter planner receives the answer to an applicant's complicated question from a superior. (An answer to a question, believed to come from the gods.) *R. Stephens*

ordinance Mandatory custom that interferes with liberty. *W. Ballbach* Bureaucratic bombardment. *E.M. Vargas*

organic disposition of elements Design in which nothing aligns with anything else on the property. *M. Roos AICP*

orphan lot [See "lot"]

OSEPA Outside Semi-Enclosed Play Area. *Pseudodictionary*

OSHA A protective coating made by half-baking a mixture of fine print, red tape, split hairs and baloney— usually applied at random with a shotgun. (Occupational Safety and Health Administration) *Nevada Nut & Bolt, Inc.*

OTE [See "OBE"]

ottoman Furniture pun for a 'chair' who is stepped on by the public or other commissioners. Even more derogatory, 'footstool.' Sometimes presides over an "Ottoman Empire." *R. Stephens* [See "chair"]

outfrastructure Facilities which are redundant or badly underperforming. Related to "outage" for supply interruption. *P. Tynan* [See "infrastructure"]

outhouse Natural amenity unit. *W. Lutz*

ozoner Drive-in movie theater. *D. Hayden*

P

pablumia A universal name for urban communities whose ambiances of uniqueness and regional flavor have been eradicated in favor of cookie cutter chain retail stores, restaurants, background music, entertainment and interchangeable local residents all dressed as Americans. The word is from the baby food, Pablum, which has a bland consistency and is completely tasteless. *C. Lesko* [See "custard development" and "architectural style"]

Painted Ladies [See "architectural style"]

Palace of Puzzles 1) Capitol. *D. Walters* 2) City Hall. *Anon.*

palette The range of building colors, materials, and landscaping for a project. Originally, a board, typically with a hole for the thumb, which an artist can hold while painting and on which colors are mixed. Now part of common 'designer-babble.' *Anon.* [See "color code" and "designer babble"]

panelized home [See "factory-built home"]

panoptic shopping center Typology of shopping center adequate to be inserted in degraded social context, since it guarantees the absolute security of the shop owners with respect to a violent clientele. *A. Haagen*

panstereorama A relief map of a town or country. *H.F. Byrne*

pantechnicon 1. A large moving van. (British) *P. Tutt* 2) A depository or place where all sorts of manufactured articles are collected for sale. *Anon.*

paper street A street that has never been built shown on an approved plan, subdivision plat, tax maps, or official map. *H. Moskowitz*

paper trail CYA documentary. *R. Stephens*

Papierkrieg Paper war. (German) Red tape dispensed en masse. *Anon.* [Paper airplanes: *Papier-luftwaffe*]

papyrus Any document produced on paper—from the reedlike material used by Egyptian scribes. *J. Horvath*

parapublic planner A planner working in both the private and public sectors at the same time. *R. Stephens*

park [See center/park]

park, natural A picturesque parcel of landscaping set aside by cities for use by muggers, drug dealers, squirrels and habitual sex offenders. *R. Bayan*
Developer: Exacted area in least developable portion of site
Environmentalist: Habitat subject to human intrusion
Fire Department: Fuel depot

Parks Department: Lost opportunity for another softball field
Planner: Open Space
Police Department: Criminal haven/heaven
Realtor: Marginal Land
Sociologist: Passive leisure environment
Common: A place unsafe for children by day and humans by night.
R. Stephens

park planning [rule of thumb] 3-5 acres of park land per 1,000 residents. *Quimby Act Standards*

park planning rule of quadrupling [rule of thumb] Park sizes quadruple at each level of service. *R. Stephens*
- TOT LOT ~1 acre park for 250 residents
- NEIGHBORHOOD PARK 5-acre park for 1,000 residents
- COMMUNITY PARK 20-acre park for 4,000 residents
- CITYWIDE OR DISTRICT PARK ~80-acre park for +16,000 residents

parkers, mall The four main species of mall parkers: "search and destroyers," "lay and wait," "stalkers" and "see it and take it." Search and destroyers roam the aisles, cruising endlessly for the perfect spot. Lay and wait parkers position themselves at the end of an aisle and wait for a space to open up in what they start to believe is their territory. Stalkers, the most predatory, slowly follow shoppers leaving the store back to their parking spot. The favored method is to see it and take it, where shoppers don't care how far they have to walk. [See "parking"] *R. Palermo*

parking
HOLLYWOOD A free parking space directly in front of the place you want to visit.

OUTFIELD Distant parking areas. Example: "Play the outfield. Outlying areas have more spaces, lighter traffic and a lower risk of collision." *AAA*

PRIMERO The ultimate parking space. The parking space as close to the door as possible, not to be confused with first available spot. *M. Ionfield*

PRINCESS Excellent parking space(s). *SlangSite*

WILDCAT Illegal parking. *P. Tutt*

[See "parkers, mall" and "splace"]

parking cars [rule of thumb] One acre will park a hundred cars. *E. Mankin*

parking lot Where we spend a quarter of an hour searching for a well-situated space so that we can avoid walking sixty seconds to the mall entrance. *R. Bayan*

parking lot planning [rule of thumb] If you are designing a parking lot, plan on three hundred square feet per vehicle. *D. Meengs*

parking pattern, nine per cent [rule of thumb] Very simple—when the area devoted to parking is too great, it destroys the land. Do not allow more than 9 per cent of the land in any given area to be used for parking. *C. Alexander*

parking space size [rule of thumb]
COMPACT Minimum 7.5 feet wide by 16 feet long. Based on the faulty assumption that modern cars were becoming smaller. *E.M. Vargas*

HANDICAPPED Minimum 13 feet wide by 19 feet long. *M Davidson*

MODEL or DELUXE 10 feet wide by 20 feet long. *A. Davies*

STANDARD Minimum 8.5 feet wide by 18 feet long. *California Planning Roundtable*

Parking Sin's Disease Cramped parking lot resulting in tremor-like driving. *J. Stephens*

parking standards, maximum Restriction in the amount of parking to reduce vehicle trips and associated environmental impacts.

Parkinson's Fifth Law If there is a way to delay an important decision, the good bureaucracy, public or private, will find it. *Anon.*

parkway Area for driving [See "driveway"]. *R. Atkinson*

parsley around the architectural pig Landscape architecture. *C. Franklin*

parterre A building site. *H.F. Byrne*

participartational Participative. *Pseudodictionary*

paseo 1) Plannerese for 'walkway.' *R. Stephens* [See "public hearings/meetings"]

past its sell-by date 1) Outmoded or useless master plan. 2) Expired General Plan. *R. Stephens*

pastiche Fake, or a direct copy, something utterly unimaginative. *Prince Charles* [See "authentic"]

patage Patio-type sitting area created inside of a garage. *Pseudodictionary* [See "cul-de-sac cave"]

patron saints Patron saints are chosen as special protectors or guardians over areas of life.

ANIMALS St. Francis of Assisi [See "animals"]

ACHITECTS St. Thomas

ARTISTS St. Catherine of Bologna

BUILDERS St. Vincent Ferrer

CIVIL SERVANTS St. Thomas More

COMPUTERS, COMPUTER USERS, INTERNET St. Isidore of Seville

COUNCILMEN Nicholas von Flue

ECOLOGISTS, ECOLOGY St. Francis of Assisi [See "environmentalist"]

EDUCATION St. Martin de Porres

ENGINEERS St. Ferdinand III of Castile

INQUISITORS St. Peter of Verona

LANDSCAPE ARCHITECTS (gardeners) St. Fiacre

LAWYERS St. Thomas More

MOTORWAYS St. John the Baptist

NEIGHBORHOOD WATCH St. Sebastian

ORATORS St. John Chrysostom

PARKS, PARK SERVICES St. John Gualbert

PLANNERS, PUBLIC SECTOR (civil servants) St. Thomas More

PLANNERS, PRIVATE SECTOR (advocates) St. Ives

POLITICIANS St. Thomas More

REALTORS St. Joseph

ROAD BUILDERS St. Sebastian of Aparicio

RURAL COMMUNITIES St. Isidore the Farmer [See "rural country"]

SCHOOLS St. Thomas Aquinas

SCIENTISTS St. Albert the Great

SURVEYORS St. Thomas

TEACHERS St. John Baptist de la Salle
TELECOMMUNICATIONS St. Gabriel the Archangel [See "cell towers"]
TRANSPORTATION St. Christopher
ZOOS St. Francis of Assisi [See "zoo"]

patroonship Vast estate. (historic) *J. Kunstler*

pavement In Britain the footway is also called the 'pavement', in the USA the 'sidewalk'. *P. Tutt*

pavement deficiency A pothole. *J. Garreau*

pavilion The Roman military tent was often called *taberna*, a term that usually denoted a shop, because, like the shop, it was generally constructed of boards. (This word was also the source of *tavern*, since many Roman shops sold wine and served as inns. It is also the source of *tabernacle*, which, as Latin *tabernaculum*, meant a little tent, a hut.) But for non-military purposes in which a structure of less permanent nature was needed for protection against sun or rain, the Romans were accustomed to stretch a many-hued cloth, somewhat like an awning, over upright poles. Under it, in hot weather, they sometimes ate the morning or midday meal. This brilliant cloth structure, when fully spread, looked not unlike a mammoth butterfly with outspread wings; so they named it *papilio*, the Latin name of that pretty creature. Through later centuries such temporary structures found increasing use in France; its name was corrupted to *pavilon*, however, and in this form it passed into England. Our present spelling, *pavilion*, arose in the seventeenth century. *C. Funk*

PCON [pronounced 'pee con'] Personal Convenience Or Necessity. Finding required to permit alcohol sales. *K. Gonzales* [See "liquor license limit"]

peacock To acquire the best pieces of land in such a way that the surrounding land is useless to others. (Australian) *Probert Encyclopaedia*

pearl necklace Graphic appearance of street trees on a map or plan. (cartography) *A. Davies*

ped-x Pedestrian crossing. *SlangSite*

pedentary To lead a lifestyle that requires walking. (sedentary) *SlangSite*

pedestrian 1) The variable [and audible] part of the roadway for an automobile. *A. Bierce* 2) A pedestrian is a man in danger of his life; a walker is a man in possession of his soul. *D. McCord*

pedestrian furniture Park benches. *J. Leach*

pedestrian-oriented Doesn't have enough parking. *Glass Steel and Stone*

pedestrian pockets A mixed-use community that stresses walking and bicycling instead of parking lots and the automobile. *B. Inman*

pedistrate To walk. From the word 'pedestrian.' *Pseudodictionary*

peds and pedal pushers Pedestrians and cyclists. *R. Stephens*

pendulum effect Policy moves from one extreme to another in a continuous cycle of reaction to the negative consequences of decisions. Council hearing chambers become

'The Pit and the Pendulum.' *R. Stephens*

penturb Another name for edge city. The term derives from the five migrations of the American people, beginning with the north-south migration on the East Coast in colonial times and culminating with the fifth migration, the move to edge cities. Another association is to the Pentagon, which, when built, was an enormous amount of office space in a rural setting. *J. Garreau* [See "edge city"]

People's Republic of ____ [See "city"]

percussive maintenance The fine art of whacking the crap out of an electronic device to get it to work again. *Anon.*

Perelman's Point There is nothing like a good painstaking survey full of decimal points and guarded generalizations to put a glaze like a Sung vase on your eyeball. *S. Perelman* [See "MEGO"]

periegesis A description of an area. H.F. Byrne

permaculture Permanent agriculture— concerned with sustainable agriculture and community living. *B. Mollison*

personal water craft (PWC) Plannerese for 'kayak,' 'canoe,' 'jet ski' etc. *R. Stephens*

persons of longevity [See "demographics"]

pet resort 'Vacation suites' for boarding pets. Some luxury pet resorts have antique furnishings, beauty parlors, bone-shaped pools, bottled water, condos, cottages, family rooms, fleeced beds, furniture (i.e. chairs and couches), gourmet meals, grooming and massage facilities (including 'peticures'), spa services, suites, themed areas (i.e. The Magic Kingdom), TV/VCR, valet services. *R. Stephens* Pet resort names include: Bed and Biscuit, Canine Country Club, Club Pet, Kitty Condo, Pet Palace, Petropolis, etc.

petition proliferation Gathering petition signatures like amassing or storing ammunition in the belief that the side with the larger petition 'arsenal' is guaranteed victory. Also, 'petition stockpiling.' *R. Stephens* [See "weapon of mass distraction"]

photoshopaganda Graphic propaganda. *R. Stephens*

photoshoplifting Swiping images from the web and appropriating them in your own work. *Pseudodictionary*

photoslop Lame or awful Photoshop work. *Pseudodictionary*

PI Public Information. Planning dispensed "over the counter." *Anon.*

piñata [See "house"]

pioneer buyers Home buyers who endure mega-commutes for a shot at affordable housing. *B. Inman*

pipeline Flow of information usually from advisors to decision-makers. A good planner is similar to "Mr. Plumber" and a poor planner requires "Mr. Plunger." *E.M. Vargas*

Pit-stop America When strip commercial serves special markets. *G. Clay*

placebo A place that has the appearance, but none of the value of a real place. *R. Stephens*

place-making New-age planning. *R. Stephens*

plan Angle, big idea, gag, hustle, lay, moves, racket, ropes, scam, schmeer, wangle, wheeze. *J. Green*

plan, to To bother about the best method of accomplishing an accidental result. *A. Bierce*

Plan A 'The' plan. The pre-geopolitical plan. *R. Stephens*

Plan B An alternate plan of action, when your original plan starts to crash and burn Example: "Okay, let's get plan B into motion..." *SlangSite*

Plan C The Compromise plan after plans A and B are rejected. Often the most Characterless. *R. Stephens*

Plan your dive. Dive your plan. Implementation must follow planning. (SCUBA) *M. Winogrond AICP* [See "sports analogies"]

planarchy Rule by a plan.

plandemonium Planning department. *R. Stephens*

planecdote A brief staff presentation of a case. *R. Stephens*

planectomy A surgical procedure to amend a plan to remove controversial policies, standards or requirements. *R. M. Robinson AICP*

planesthesia [See "MEGO"]

planeuver Planning management with address or artful design; an adroit procedure; intrigue; stratagem. *R. Stephens*

planette Small plan, planling. "Make no planettes."

planic Plan + panic. *A. Morse*

planicide [See "DBT" and "DBTD/DBTN"]

planimony [See "married to a plan"]

planna wannabe Pseudo-planner. From 'I want to be a planner.' *R. Esteban*

plannage That which is associated with planners and planning. *R. Stephens*

planneous Partaking of the nature of planning, or abounding with or formed by it; plannery. *C. Chipping*

planner 1) A navigator responsible for sailing the ship to the correct port despite hurricanes, calm seas, other ships, lack of steering equipment and instruments, and under the command of numerous captains who may not agree as to the heading, tack or even correct port. A multiple noun [i.e. <u>den</u> of thieves, <u>deck</u> of cards, <u>school</u> of fish, etc.] for planners is a 'plot' or 'place' of planners. *R. Stephens* 2) Having acquired a little knowledge about a lot of things in school, the planner continues to learn less and less about more and more until eventually the planner knows nothing about everything. This contrasts with the engineer who learns a lot about a very few things and eventually knows everything about nothing— a situation which makes for interesting working relationships between the two disciplines. *Private Planning Perspectives* 3) A Planner is a person who, given 2+2, will arrive at a range somewhere between 3½ and 4½. *J. Freiman* 4) A planner is an individual who collects incomplete information from unreliable sources, then uses it to draw a mathematically precise line from an unwarranted assumption to a politically predetermined position. *C. Baker* 5) Developer/Council fodder. *Dear Mary, The Dispatch*

planner convention "He's got a great idea...I'm glad I thought of it." *R. Castillo*

planner, urban (international)

ARABIC	Mahandes Baladiat
ARMENIAN	Kahakashinarar
BRITISH	Town Planner
BULGARIAN	Gradski planosnimach
CHINESE	Tu Sur Si Chi Su
DANISH	Byplanlaegger
DUTCH	Stedebouwkundige, Planoloog
FRENCH	Urbaniste
GERMAN	Stadtplaner
HUNGARIAN	Város Tervezo
ITALIAN	Urbanista
JAPANESE	Toshi keikaku ka

KOREAN	Dosi Sulgesa
MALAYSIAN	Perancang
NIGERIAN [Igbo]	Odozi Obodo
PERSIAN [Farsi]	Mohandes Shahrsazi
POLISH	Urbanistow
PORTUGUESE	Urbanista
RUSSIAN	Gradastraitel
SANSKRIT	Vastu Shastri
SOUTH AFRICAN	Streekbeplanner
SPANISH	Urbanista
THAI	Pung Meong
TURKISH	Sehir Planlamag_

planner taxonomy
AUTOMATIC or MANUAL Public or Private
BRICKS & STICKS Urban & Regional
IMPORTED or DOMESTIC Contract or Staff
NEAR-SIGHTED, FAR-SIGHTED, or BLIND Current, Advanced, or Administrative
PLANNERISTE or PLANOLOGIST Artistic or Analytic *R. Stephens*
TOWN & COUNTRY Urban & Regional (British)

plannerese 1) The language of plannage, in a planner of speaking. *R. Stephens* 2) Planner patois. *Los Angeles Times Magazine* 3) Plannerspeak. *Times Magazine* 4) planning paladic (British) *Anon.*

plannerism A personal and prominent peculiarity of style in planning. *Anon.*

Planner's Buzz Word System [PBWS] A system of three columns of "buzz" words which may be randomly combined to generate phrases for use in presentations and reports for "that ring of decisive knowledgeable authority". *D. Winterbottom MRAPI*

Column 1	Column 2	Column 3
0 Integrated	0 Management	0 Options
1 Regional	1 Planning	1 Flexibility
2 Equitable	2 Monitored	2 Connection
3 Quality	3 Community	3 Audit
4 Functional	4 Digital	4 Impact
5 Responsive	5 Neighborhood	5 Concept
6 Optional	6 Environmental	6 Statement
7 Comprehensive	7 Sustainable	7 Participation
8 Compatible	8 Consultative	8 Recycling
9 Balanced	9 Policy	9 Strategy

Guides to impressive but fuzzy words are known by a number of names including "The Baffle-Gab Thesaurus," "The Buzz Phrase Projector," and "The Handy Obfuscator". *P. Dickson*

planner's palette [See "color code/convention"]

planners, patron saint of [See "patron saints"]

planning 1) The ancient arts of fortune-telling, finger-painting and alchemy folded no larger than 8½ x 11 inches. 2) Planning truly is in the eyes of the beholder! Planning to the council person is bending the rules to stay on the Council. To the commissioner it is bending the rules to see if they can get onto the Council. Planning is a "poor cousin" to the architect. Planning is "Rosemary's baby" to the engineer. Planning is the "light at the end of the tunnel" for planners. This explains why many planners have "tunnel vision"! *Dear Mary* in "The Dispatch" 3) Land Use ---, Interior decorators gone wild. *R. Castillo* 4) A boutique service [as perceived by some engineering firms]. *S. McCutchan AICP* 5) [See Wolf's Planning Law]. *C. Wolf, Jr.* 6) The longer ahead you plan a special event, and the more special it is, the more likely it is to go wrong [The [F]law of Long-Range Planning]. *D. Evelyn* 7) The restriction of development. A reactive rather than proactive process seeking to regulate the use of land and buildings, carried out by planning officials or planners. *R. Holder*

planning ahead [rule of thumb] You can think ahead half your age. *G. Gappert*

Planning Department   Official Doublespeak for a Subdivision and Building Approval Department which does no genuine planning whatsoever. Planning requires looking at least a lifespan into the future. Some believe the foresight should be seven generations. Yet there is little evidence of any "Planning" Department looking farther in the future than about 4 weeks - which coincides with the maximum delay to the meeting where some body of elected officials will give final approval without asking substantial questions providing more evidence for the "political gap." *Helping Our Peninsula's Environment*

planning director / pope What is the difference between the Pope and the Planning Director? With the Pope, You only have to kiss his ring! *B. Inman*

planning for dummies [See "smart"]

planning junkies [See "public hearing/meeting participants"]

planning mascot   Penguin. Formal appearing bird having rudimentary wings useless for flight, but effective in swimming. The term of venery is a 'colony of penguins.' [See "terms of venery"]

planning posse Close planning friends, department or gang. *R. Stephens*

Planning Prime Directive [See "health, safety and welfare"]

planning prince/princess A planner suffering from delusions of royalty. *J. Stephens*

planning staff
EXECUTIVE DIRECTOR Leaps tall buildings with a single bound. Is more powerful than a locomotive. Is faster than a speeding bullet. Walks on water. Makes policy.
PLANNING DIRECTOR Leaps short buildings with a single bound. Is more powerful than a switch engine. Is just as fast as a speeding bullet. Walks on water if the sea is calm.
CHIEF PLANNER Leaps short buildings with a running start and a tail wind. Is almost as powerful as a switch engine. Is faster than a speeding beebee. Walks on water in indoor swimming pools. Discusses policy if special request is approved.
SENIOR PLANNER Barely clears Quonset huts. Loses tug-of-war with locomotives. Can fire a speeding bullet. Swims well. Occasionally hears about policy.
REGIONAL PLANNER Makes high marks when trying to leap buildings. Is run over by locomotives. Can sometimes handle guns without inflicting self injury. Dog paddles. Knows policy exists.
PLANNING TECHNICIAN Runs into buildings. Recognizes locomotives two out of three. Is not issued ammunition. Can stay afloat if properly instructed in use of Mae West. Pays premiums on policy.
PUBLIC PARTICIPATION COORDINATOR Falls over doorsteps when trying to enter building. Says "look at the choo-choo." Wets himself with a water pistol. Plays in mud puddles. Can't afford policy.

OFFICE SECRETARY Lifts buildings and walks under them. Kicks locomotives off track. Catches speeding bullets in teeth and eats them. Freezes water with a single glance. Explains policy to Executive Director.
Dr. J. Segedy AICP

planning students Closet Utopians. *H. Jacobs* [See "studentia"]

planning theme song Scars and Stripes Forever. *J. Freiman AICP*

planning, urban (international)

BRITISH	town planning
FRENCH	plan d'occupation des sols (POS)
GERMAN	Stadtplanung
ITALIAN	planificazione urbana
SPANISH	planificación urbanistica

plannoid[al] Resembling a plan. Example: "That project was so poorly designed, it wasn't even plannoidal." *R. Stephens*

planocracy Government by a plan.

planoholic Addiction to planning.

planolatry Worship of plans. Example: "The General (Master) Plan is the planning bible and the Council practices planolatry." *M. Reed*

planology The science of planning as opposed to planning art—'objets de Plan' by an urbaniste. This is the reason for so much Plannerese—the attempt to make planning expressions more 'scientific.' *R. Stephens*

planomancy Divination based on a plan. Black magic associated with the interpretation of "bubble diagrams" for General and Master Plans. *R. Stephens* [See "bubble diagram"]

planomania Obsession with planning. Phenomenon most commonly observed during the period immediately preceding deadlines and public hearings. *R. Stephens* [See "PPS"]

planomatic A boiler plate planning document used by a consultant to prepare an "individualized" plan for one city by just changing the name of the last city which employed the consultant. *R. M. Robinson AICP*

planophilia Love of a plan. Example: "Where's the love? Just look at the planophilia for the new Master Plan Update." *R. Stephens*

planophobia Strong aversion to planning regulation common among both developers and no-growth activists. *R. Stephens*

Planopoly Board game with standard land uses. *R. Stephens*
plantastico Plan + fantastic. *A. Gomez*

planter What everyone thinks you said when asked what you do. *D. Bess AICP*

planthology A collection of selected plans, most commonly the "alternatives" listed alphabetically, or in complex/expensive programs, listed by roman numerals. *R. Stephens*

Planungvergnügen The joy of planning. (German) *M. Schrenk*

planus The fundamental plan. *R. Stephens*

platitude Map with an attitude. *R. Stephens*

Platlantis Subdivision within a flood plain. *R. Stephens*

platulence Noxious gases from an obnoxious map. *R. Stephens*

players, actors, stars Powerful [often theatrical] decision-makers. *A. Bell AICP* [See "public hearing/meeting participants]

plex Movie cinema featuring multiple screens; short for multiplex. *K. Watts* [See "center/park" and "cineplex"]

plot plan A map showing the developer's burial ground. *R. Granados*

plottage Connected plots; a collective term for more than one plot of land, which collection for one reason or another has its own distinct identity and value. *D.E. Miller*

plottage value Increase in value resulting from the combining of two adjacent properties. *Kenneth Leventhal & Company*

plug and chug Planning and implementation. *R. D. Hulme*

plunk art 1) Artwork plunked in place once the building and its landscaping are done. *P. Suter* 2) Abstract sculptures placed about a development for reasons that are an utter mystery ("plop art"). *J. Garreau*

pluripotent Not fixed as to developmental potentialities; having developmental plasticity. *B. Clark*

PMS Post Meeting Syndrome. Frustration or anger resulting from meetings. *R. Stephens* [See "public hearing/meeting"]

POD 1) Planner Of the Day. Person manning the public counter and phones. This is a sentence, not an award. *M. Roos AICP* 2) Pedestrian Oriented Development

pod An area of single-use zoning (such as a shopping center or residential subdivision) located off a major road. *D. Hayden*

podmall Also known as a convenience center, the podmall is a small shopping center with a few small stores and a small parking lot. It answers basic shopping needs in densely populated urban areas whose large shopping centers have moved out into the suburbs. *H. Lemay* [See "shopping mall"]

policy [See "assumptions"]

policy statement A pronouncement written in vague terms which can be interpreted to fit the prevailing mood. *J. Hingtgen* [See "assumptions"]

Polishing the Cartographic Image, Eleven Rules for [rule of thumb] (How to Lie with Maps)

1. Be shrewdly selective.
2. Frame strategically
3. Accentuate the positive
4. If caught, have a story ready
5. Minimize the negative
6. Dazzle with detail
7. Persuade with pap
8. Distract with aerial photographs and historical maps
9. Generalize creatively
10. Enchant with elegance
11. When all else fails, try [institutional] bribery

M. Monmonier [See "magic of miniaturizaton"]

political asylum Council chambers. *R. Stephens*

Political Effectiveness (Rule of Thumb) One's political effectiveness is generally inversely related to the number of things one can name in Latin. [Note: For potential activists who need some Latin words, here are some: *Nonnulli tam intellegentes sunt ut stulti sint* ("Some people are so smart, they're stupid.").] *J. Britell*

political planning [rule of thumb] People moving into a new tract development are politically inert for five years. *G. Evans*

politically correct [POCO, PC] "Multi-culturalism" or an emphasis on social justice. *H. Henderson*

politico Politician. D. Hageman

pollutician   A politician who supports initiatives and policies that harm the environment. *Orange County Register*

Po-Mo Short for postmodern. *K. Moloney* [See "architecture, modern"]

Ponderosa, The [See "lot" and "subdivision scale"]

popullution Pollution caused by excess population. Example: "The citizens of large cities suffer from the effects of popullution." *SlangSite*

pork chop lot [See "lot"]

porte cochere Large doorway allowing vehicles to drive into or through a building. (architecture) *Probert Encyclopaedia*

post-consumer secondary materials Garbage. *W. Lutz*

postage stamp lot [See "lot"]

posy-sniffers [See "environmentalist"]

potable Drinkable. *Anon.*

Potemkin Village A façade depicting false prosperity. From the name of Russian Empress Catherine the Great's prime minister, who erected these facades complete with singing festive peasants along the Volga River from her Summer Palace so that she could see from her barge that rumors of her disgruntled starving people were unfounded. *J. Parker*

pourparler An informal conference. *H.F. Byrne*

PowderPoint presentation A puffy or poofy slideshow. *R. Stephens*

power center A large, open-air retail mall that consists mostly of big-box stores. *M. Glover* [See "big box"]

PowerPoint poisoning Nauseous state of mind and body induced by attending "professional" presentations. Can be fatal when exposed to the full range of bells 'n' whistles. Milder doses induce resignation, lassitude and apathy. *M. Rodent*

PPS Pre Proposal Syndrome. A condition characterized by nervousness, irritability, emotional instability, depression and possibly headaches; it occurs during the 7 to 10 days before a proposal deadline and disappears a few hours after the deadline. *N. Victor*

prairie dogging When someone yells or drops something loudly in a 'cube farm' and everyone's heads pop up over the walls to see what's going on. [See "animals" and "cube farm"]

pre-cut home [See "factory-built home"]

prenup Pre-annexation Agreement. *R. Stephens*

preplanning Planning. *P. Dickson*

presentate To make a presentation. *J. Evert*

princess parking [See "parking"]

private sector Real world of business or private enterprise, or anything outside of government; also known as; 'public sector.' *K. Watts*. [See "CREAM" and "public sector"]

privatopia A walled-in or gated community of private homes, especially one in which a homeowner association establishes and enforces rules related to property appearance and resident behavior. *D. Krueckeberg* [See "gated community"]

proactive Advance planning. *P. Dickson*

procedural safeguards Red tape. *D.E. Miller*

product Everything in a development that was put there by the hand of man. Whether it be a parking lot, a curbing, a planting of flowers, or a high-rise, somebody views it as Product, and can go into astounding detail about whether it is good or bad, cheap or expensive. *J. Garreau*

proffers The system of legalized extortion by which governments convince developers "voluntarily" to build such socially desirable facilities as ball fields, day-care centers, schools, and intersections, in exchange for the governmental unit being kind enough to give the developer permission to build at higher density than usual or, sometimes, to give him approval to build at all. *J. Garreau* [See "exaction" and "impact fee"]

program Any assignment that takes more than one phone call to complete. *S. Young*

programmed space   A place where a spontaneous expression of community is thought to be so unlikely that a consultant has to be paid to hire a street musician to play. *J. Garreau* [See "animated space"]

project manager   The conductor of an orchestra in which every musician is in a different union.

project phases
1.   Enthusiasm & exultation
2.   Disillusionment & disenchantment
3.   Panic & confusion
4.   Search for the Guilty
5.   Punishment of the Innocent
6.   Praise and Honors for the Non Participants.
Anon. [See "public hearing phases"]

property owner's manual   Zoning code. *R. Stephens*

Property Rights, Basic rule of   If a property owner ever had the right to urinate on a piece of property, he has a perpetual right to site a toxic outfall on that same property. Asserting rights over one's private property is All-American: asserting public interest over public property is un-American. *J. Britell*

protectorate   Sphere of influence. A relationship of protection and partial control assumed by a county over a dependent unincorporated town or area. *R. Stephens* [See "annexoria nervosa," "fear of influence" and "Lebensraum"]

prunewhip [See "architectural ornamentation"]

pseudo-city [See "city"]

pseudo-community New urbanist community. *R. Sennett*

psychogeography The study of the precise effects of geographical setting, consciously managed or not, acting directly on the mood and behavior of the individual. *Internationale Situationniste*

PUBLIC People United for Better Living in Cities.

public hearing/meeting 1) Time for a long, boring presentation by a developer. Presentation must include: a long list of consultants, models, charts, graphs, maps, renderings, photographs, and other displays. Followed by a discussion period, which gives citizens a chance to attack the developer's business sense, æsthetic judgement, and parentage. *D. Ring* 2) An event in America where no one listens. *D. Kemmis* [See "Triple Crown"]
311 Indecent exposure to the public. (police code) *A. Jones*
AIRDANCE Official speaking on a position without any support. (hanging) *R. Stephens*
AMATEUR NIGHT Karaoke without the music. *R. Stephens*
AUTO-DA-FÉ A public, solemn or reverent rite or ceremony, formerly held by the courts of the Inquisition at the execution of heretics condemned to the stake. [See "planning hearing/meeting, nobody expects the Spanish Inquisition"]
BUNS OF STEEL Interminable city council meetings. "Got to go, I'm late for Buns of Steel." *T. Baker*
CHEAP THEATRE *D. Bess AICP*

CIRCUS MINIMUS Minor spectacle. *R. Stephens*

CLIFFHANGER Unresolved and suspenseful continued hearing. *R. Stephens*

COMA TOES More severe than 'buns of steel,' 'fanny fatigue' or having your leg 'fall asleep.' *R. Stephens*

DAYS OF OUR LIVES Televised melodramatic soap opera. *R. Stephens*

DIALOGUE OF THE DEAF *R. Cole*

DOG AND PONY SHOW Formal presentation aimed at gathering support for a system or issue. Visuals [usually projected on a screen], handouts, and large graphs are essential to a true dog-and-pony show. *P. Dickson*

ENCHANTED TIKI ROOM Parroting, robotic speakers often speaking simultaneously. *R. Stephens*

ENCORE Speakers who return to the podium to add further testimony. *R. Stephens*

FANNY FATIGUE The soreness you develop in your bum caused by the seats. *SlangSite*

FIVE BY FIVE Unanimous vote. (aerospace) *R. Stephens*

FLYING DUTCHMAN Public hearing case doomed to continuation because the applicant is absent. *R. Stephens*

HALF-TIME SHOW *P. Dickson*

HEARING FROM HELL *E. Costello AICP*

HEARTILAGE To seek pity or preferential treatment because of something that emotionally effects you. *F.Weir*

HELLUVA RIDE A difficult ride from the point of view as a rider or being ridden. *J. Stephens*

INTERMISSION A period of hearing 'advertisements' when those giving testimony provide information related to their organization or business. *R. Stephens*

JUMP THE SHARK The precise moment when you know the project has lost political support. (From the TV show episode when Fonzie jumped over a shark on water skis. After this episode, the show went downhill.) *Pseudodictionary*

LASERIUM Multiple presenters simultaneously using laser pointers. *R. Stephens* [See "Jedi Knight"]

LET'S MAKE A DEAL   Game show negotiations especially with Development Agreements. *R. Stephens*

MEETINGCIDE Death, typically by boredom, due to the frequency of meetings or the length of a single meeting. Example: "Meetingcide was the clear cause of Rebecca's death due to the ridiculous amount of time she spent in the staff meetings required by the organization." *Sem & Rel*

MIDNIGHT TO MOANING Hearings lasting past midnight. *R. Stephens*

MODERN DAY FIRING SQUAD *R. Castillo*

MONTHLY MELODRAMA Complete with drama queens and kings. *Anon.*

NOBODY EXPECTS THE SPANISH INQUISITION!   Cardinal Ximinez of Spain (Michael Palin): NOBODY expects the Spanish Inquisition! Our chief weapon is surprise...surprise and fear...fear and surprise.... Our two weapons are fear and surprise...and ruthless efficiency.... Our *three* weapons are fear, surprise, and ruthless efficiency...and an almost fanatical devotion to the [Mayor].... Our *four*...no... *Amongst* our weapons.... Amongst our weaponry...are such elements as fear, surprise.... I'll come in again. *Monte Python*

PARAKROUSIS When a single public official votes contrary to the hearing body. The striking of a slightly wrong note in an otherwise tuneful harmony (Greek). *C. Dexter*

THE PIT AND THE PENDULUM [See "pendulum effect"]

PUBLIC CONSTIPATION Clogged up participatory system. *Anon.*

QUALITY TIME Design Review Board hearing. *R. Stephens*

REBUTTAL REDUX/REBUFF Returning to the podium to add to or contradict the closing rebuttal. *R. Stephens*

REBUTTAL REVERSAL Applicant's rebuttal at a public hearing that does more damage than repair. *R. Stephens*

RED HEARING (red herring) A hearing item that draws attention away from the main issue. *R. Stephens*

SÉANCE 'I see dead people.' *R. Stephens*

SHOW & TELL Revealing analysis. Also, 'open kimono.' *R. Stephens*

SLOW MOTION REPLAY Slowly repeating the motion to clarify, persuade or pontificate. *R. Stephens*

SONG AND DANCE American vaudeville performers who, coming upon the stage, open the act with a song and follow it with a dance. *C. Funk*

STADIUM SCENES FROM BEN HUR *R. Castillo*

TEOTWAWKI The End Of The World As We Know It. *SlangSite*

UNDER THE BIG TENT Circus performance. *R. Stephens*

VOMITORIUM Getting it all out in the open. *R. Stephens*

public hearing/meeting participants

ACADEMY AWARD NOMINEE Someone giving a dramatic presentation, often from reading a script.

ALL HANDS ON BOARD Quorum and/or unanimous voters. *R. Stephens* [See "man overboard"]

BACKGROUND SINGERS Supporters of a project advocate. *S. Preston FAICP*

BANSHEES Members of the audience who emit audible sighs, gasps, groans, moans, etc. after testimony from the opposition. [In Gaelic belief, a banshee was female entity who heralds a death by groaning and screaming.]

BARON/BARONESS Public official enjoying power and influence over his/her fellow officials. *N. Jones*

FREQUENT FLYER Consultant who regularly attends public hearings on numerous different cases.

GM (general manager), GAME-MASTER, GAVEL-MASTER, GRUPPENMEISTER... Chair. *R. Stephens*

HEARING GROUPIE Someone who regularly attends public meetings and hearings with or without interest in any particular agenda items. Also, 'planning junkie.'

HEKAWI TRIBE Confused citizen's group. From the 'F Troop' television show 'We're the Hekawi.' (Where the heck are we?) *R. Stephens*

JEERLEADER One who leads the jeering. *Pseudodictionary*

MAN OVERBOARD Dissenting voter. *R. Stephens* [See 'all hands on board']

MEETNIK A person who enjoys meetings and all sorts of administrative events and tries to attend as many of them as possible. *M. Epstein*

MOBSTACLE A crowd that blocks passage. *Nonesuch*

PEANUT GALLERY The hindmost seating section and/or a group of people whose opinions are considered unimportant. *Anon.*

PERP WALK The parade of consultants or other speakers. (criminal justice) *R. Stephens*

PLANNING JUNKIES People who attend all public hearings. *K. King*

PLANNING PASEO Grand entrance of the public officials or the project team to the hearing chambers. (In bullfighting, the formal procession into the ring of the players, including the matadors, banderilleros, and horses, that occurs just before the first bull is fought.) *Dictionary.com*

ROYALTY Drama queens and kings. *R. Stephens*

SAUSAGE PARTY   Where the ratio of men to women is extremely high. *Pseudodictionary*

SEAT CUSHION Meeting attendee who does not contribute. *E.M. Vargas*

SHIRLEY'S TEMPLE Young girl (sometimes used by a special interest group) giving a syrupy testimony about her home or other sacred place. *R. Stephens* [See "Tom's Lawyer"]

SINATRA Chairman of the Board who does it his way. *R. Stephens*

SIR ANTHONY Elderly man giving a Shakespearean presentation. From the actor Anthony Hopkins. Also 'Sir Lawrence' from Lawrence Olivier. *J. Stephens*

STREEP PERFORMER Woman giving an overly dramatic presentation. From the actress Merryl Streep and 'street performer.' *J. Stephens*

SUITS Professional consultants hired to provide expert testimony. *Anon.*

TOM'S LAWYER Young boy (sometimes used by a special interest group) giving a corny testimony including recitation of codes or laws. *R. Stephens* [See "Shirley's Temple"]

WRANGLER Organizer of a special interest group. *R. Stephens*

[See "environmentalist," "consultant," "hired gun," "Joe," and "special interests"]

Public Hearing Phases 1) Applicant's view: Denial, Anger, Grief, Acceptance. (fatal illness) 2) City Official's view: Enthusiasm, Confusion, Disillusionment, Numbness. *R. Stephens* [See "project phases"]

Public Hearings, The Natural Laws of [rule of thumb]

Law 1: The length of the hearing is in inverse proportion to the comfort of the chair.

Law 2: The length of the argument is in inverse proportion to the logic of points being offered. [also, the volume of the speaker's voice is in inverse proportion to the validity of the argument.]

Law 3: The number of speakers [and their comments] will always exceed the available pages in your notebook you planned to use to take notes.

Law 4: The Chairperson/Mayor will always forget to set the 3-minute timer when a friend [or ally] is speaking. Also, isn't it funny how three minutes seem to last only two minutes when an opponent is speaking?

Law 5: Someone will always ask for your item to be continued when you have prepared your presentation to the last detail—and likewise, you'll never get a continuance or postponement when you really need it! *Anon*

public-private property pendulum The continuing shift in dominance between public and private sector property rights. *R. Stephens*

public-private partnership 1) A method by which developers and governments engage in a cooperative rather than confrontational exercise in getting a development built in a fashion that mollifies the neighbors. This is seen by its advocates as the height of developer enlightenment, a Zen in which the builder works "with" the Community, recognizing that he does not really "own" the land he is paying the bank for. It is seen by its detractors as either communist horse pucky or the system by which foxes and chickens are brought together to achieve common goals. *J. Garreau* 2) Two persons who dance together. A relationship between one or more parties involving close cooperation in exercise of specific rights and responsibilities. *Southeast Tourism Society*

public sector Government—all branches, all levels, from federal to local. *K. Watts.*[See "private sector"]

public waste reception center Dump. *W. Lutz*

puff 'n' powder A purely cosmetic rehabilitation. *K. Moloney*

puffery Seller's hype about property that's sufficiently general that it does not amount to a fraudulent misstatement of fact. *Kenneth Leventhal & Company* [See "real estate ad phrases"]

puffing Exaggerating the attractions of a piece of property without actually misrepresenting it (which constitutes fraud). The line between puffing and sound salesmanship is often rather thin. *D.E. Miller*

puppet appointment Appointed city official selected to represent the view(s) of one or more City Council. *E.M. Vargas* [See "puppet mastser"]

puppet master Individual who has excessive influence over others. Also, "puppeteer." *E.M. Vargas* [See "puppet appointment"]

put on a pedestal [See "Blathering Heights"]

pyramid zoning [See "zoning].

Q

quality of life (QOL) 1) A phrase used to help describe increased traffic congestion, as in "There has been a decline in...." *D. Ring* 2) That attribute which a development is said to be sensitive to when attention is being drawn to intangibles that do not directly contribute to the bottom line. *J. Garreau* 3) What an industrialized nation is said to offer when enough of its citizens are suffering from terminal stress. *R. Bayan*

quality of life development formula [rule of thumb] Quality of life development (value) is a function of personal space (lot size, building size) and community amenities.
$\$ = DU + Bldg + A_1, A_2,...$ Where $\$$ is cost, DU is lot size, Bldg is house size, A is amenity
Example: A very small lot with golf course frontage may be comparable in value to a much larger lot without the view, or an average-sized lot with a larger house. Where land is expensive, the suburban formula focuses on maximizing building size and minimizing lot size. This formula does not hold for extreme cases. *R. Stephens* [See "less filling, more taste"]

quality statement Very large, heavy, expensive, neutral sculpture. Ideally, brushed steel or aluminum. Totally plain geometry a plus. Moving parts, and/or integration into an active water feature, daring. Located at the entrance of an office park or complex [or other large development] *J. Garreau* [See "beauty contest" and "plunk art"]

quality time [See "public hearing/meeting"]

quick and dirty Work done to meet a deadline which does not have high quality. *A. Davies*

quiet enjoyment The right to live in or enjoy the use of property without being bothered, a right guaranteed in most binding legal documents pertaining to real estate ownership. *D.E. Miller*

Quiet Revolution, The Regional Planning *J. Levy*

quorum 1) The literal meaning of this Latin word is "of whom." But, *quorum* was once part of a Latin phrase—in this instance, a legal phrase. Originally, that is, it was a custom, among English justices of the peace, to name one, or perhaps two or three, of especial knowledge or prudence and without whose presence the other justices would be unwilling or unable to proceed with the business of the court. Thus the wording of the commissions naming such a justice or justices, contained the Latin expression, "*quorum vos*, William Jones, *unum* (*duos, tres*, etc.) *esse volumus*." "Of whom we will that you, William Jones be one (two, three, etc.)." The abbreviation , quorum, was thus first applied to specified persons who were required to be present before a session could be opened, and it ultimately developed the meaning in which we now employ it, a prescribed number of the members of a group whose presence is necessary before business may be transacted. *C. Funk* 2) Minimum number of officials for a public quarrel. *R. Stephens*

quorum decorum Appropriateness of behavior or conduct by the majority of the board or agency. *R. Stephens*

QWERTY Phenomenon Practices that have an historical, but no rational, basis. *S. Papert* [The typical keyboard letters are arranged QWERTYUIOP to prevent early typewriters from jamming.]

R

rabbi Senior official who exerts influence or patronage on behalf of a person. *Probert Encyclopaedia*

rabid transit Congestion gone crazy. *H. Eng AICP*

rails to trails The program to convert abandoned railways to public trails. What the automobile failed to do to the railways, hikers and bikers are working to finish. *M. Urushibata*

rain forest Greenwash for 'jungle'. [See "jungle" and "greenwash"]

raisin ranch Retirement community. *K. Henniksen* [See "NORC"]

ranchburger [See "house"]

range Unfenced open space. (cowboy) *R. Adams*

Ranger's Rule [See "mottos"]

ratable bandwagon Approval of poor development that promises to increase the tax base. *H. Smith*

rational nexus The reasonableness of impact fees on new development by evaluating the fee against the key criteria of need, cost and benefit.

Ratzelfratzel Effect Response to complicated technology. *J. Sharbutt* [Equivalent to the symbols "@#*^%!" in comic strips]

raw land Vacant land ripe for development. Often served with half-baked development proposal based on incomplete number cooking. *R..Robinson* [See "number cooking"]

read 'em and weep When the voter board shows an undesirable vote. *R. Stephens*

real estate A small piece of the earth traded as a speculative commodity for centuries after some dead white male had the audacity to claim ownership. Each parcel commands a price based on its perceived value, so that a hundred-acre stand of spruce forest fetches roughly as much as the weed-infested lot next to a video store. *R. Bayan* [See "surreal estate"]

real estate refugees People who move out of the city and into the surrounding suburbs and towns so they can purchase a larger home on a bigger lot. *P. Nussbaum*

real estate relativity Project processing time as perceived by bureaucrats ("It doesn't matter to me"), consultants ("Time is money"), and developer/builders ("Timing is *everything*"). *R Stephens*

real estate repo Expired subdivision map. *R. Stephens*

real estate ad phrases
AND MUCH, MUCH MORE Nothing else comes to mind.
BRIGHT AND SUNNY Venetian blinds not included.
BRILLIANT CONCEPT Do you really need a two-story live oak in your 30-foot sky dome? Also 'Makes Dramatic Statement.'
CHARMING Tiny. Snow White might fit, but five of the dwarfs would have to find their own place. Also 'Cute,' 'Enchanting,' and 'Good Starter Home.'
COMFORTABLE Very small.
COMPLETELY UPDATED Avocado dishwasher and harvest gold carpeting or vice versa.
CONTEMPORARY At least 15 years old. [See "architecture, modern"]
COZY Very, very small.
DARING DESIGN Still a warehouse.
EXECUTIVE NEIGHBORHOOD High taxes.
HI-TECH/CONTEMPORARY Lots of steel shelving with little holes—the kind your dad used to store tools on in the basement. [See "architecture, modern"]
HURRY! WON'T LAST About to collapse.
LOW MAINTENANCE No lawn.
MODERN 30-40 years old. [See "architecture, modern"]
MUCH POTENTIAL Grim. Steer clear unless you have a lot of money and believe your blind dates really did have nice personalities. Also 'Ready to Rehab,' and 'Fixer

Upper.'

MUST SEE TO BELIEVE An absolutely accurate statement.

NATURAL SETTING Forget about planting, the deer will eat everything.

NEAR HOUSES OF WORSHIP Fanatical denomination next door.

OLD-FASHIONED Derelict. *R. Holder*

ONE-OF-A-KIND Ugly as sin.

PARK-LIKE SETTING A tree on the block.

PRESTIGIOUS Expensive.

SECLUDED SETTING Far away.

SOPHISTICATED Black walls and no windows. Also 'architect's delight.'

SPACIOUS Average.

SPRAWLING RANCH Inefficient floor plan. [See "architectural style"]

STARTER HOME Rundown. [See "house"]

TOWNHOUSE Former tenement.

UNAFFECTED CHARM Needs painting.

UNIQUE CITY HOME Used to be a warehouse.

UPPER BRACKET If you have to ask…

WALK TO STORES Nowhere to park.

YOU'LL LOVE IT No you won't.

rebuttal rebuff/redux [See "public hearing/meeting"]

rebuttal reversal [See "public hearing/meeting"]

rectification of frontiers The annexation of territory by force. (military) *R. Holder*
[See "annexoria nervosa," "Lebensraum" and "protectorate"]

red hearing [See "public hearing/meeting"]

red taper Bureaucrat. (British) [See "apparatchik" and "bureaucrat"] *Probert Encyclopaedia*

redevelopment "What were our predecessors thinking?" *R. Castillo*

reengineering The fundamental rethinking and radical redesign of business processes to achieve dramatic improvements in critical contemporary measures performance such as cost, quality, service, and speed. The intent of reengineering is to examine the services we offer, what services our customers want and need now and in the future, our assumptions around how service is delivered and by whom, and how we need to change in order to meet the changing business environment faced by the corporation. *Bank of America*

reg neg Short for regulatory negotiation, which is the practice of adjusting government regulations to suit an interested party. *K. Watts.*

registered relocation specialist Real estate agent. *W. Lutz*

regulations The score before tip-off. *R. Castillo* [See "sports analogies"]

replaceable places The same drive-ins, prefab motels, offices, and salesrooms on every road and corner. *G. Clay*

repo cabin [See "house"]

Request for Proposal [RFP] 1) Asking for the grocery receipt before shopping. 2) Rounding up the usual suspects. *R. Stephens* 3) Notice to bid for a government job or contract. *P. Dickson* 4) Poker game in which the losing hand wins. *Nevada Nut & Bolt. Inc.* 5) A bureaucratic formality. Before contractors can be named or grants allocated, an RFP is announced, giving all prospective contractors and applicants a chance to put in their bids. More often than not, the contractor or grantee has already been decided upon, but the RFP is used to maintain the illusion of open competition. *D.E. Miller*

reservation An area of land not taken from American Indians by white settlers. *R. Holder*

resource development park Junkyard. *W. Lutz*

resources
BIOLOGICAL RESOURCES Plannerese for plants and animals. In more picturesque times: 'flora and fauna.'
CULTURAL RESOURCES *Paleontologic* i.e. 'dino droppings.' *Archeologic* i.e. 'stones and bones'. *Historic* i.e. 'railroad tracks and shacks.' *Artistic* i.e. "murals and statues.' Their resource value is easily determined by whether or not a Museum will provide them a home. [See "stones and bones" and "artichokes"]
HUMAN RESOURCES Personnel; people.
NATURAL RESOURCES Plannerese for—basically—the whole environment
SCIENTIFIC RESOURCES Natural resources that not many people care about except scientists. I.e. Stenopelmatus intermedius, the Jerusalem cricket or potato bug.
R. Stephens

restaurant
BURGERDONALD'S A generic name for all fast food restaurants when you can't remember the one you were at, or if you have no general preference. Example:

"Where do you want to go for dinner? Eh, Burgerdonald's, doesn't matter to me. OR We heard this song the last time we were at Burgerdonald's." *SlangSite*

CHEW AND SPEW Cheap, all you can eat restaurant. *SlangSite*

COSTUME CUISINE Themed restaurants. *R. Stephens*

FROGS, DOGS, AND SAUSAGE-LOGS Foreign food. *E.M. Vargas*

GASTRIC GHETTO Restaurant row. *R. Stephens*

GASTROTURF Ghetto restaurant area. *R. Stephens*

GREASY SPOON AND BRASS SPITOON Bad restaurant with an historic "flavor." *R. Stephens*

NETCAFÉ 1) An establishment that provides a non-library study and play environment with access to computers, internet resources, and food services. Example: "I am going down to the netcafe to study. Let's go down to the netcafe and surf the internet." *SlangSite* 2) An establishment that provides a non-library study and play environment with access to computers, internet resources, and food services. *J. Bartel*

NONALD KING Any fast food burger franchise including, but not limited to, MacDonalds, Burger King, and the like. Also refers to food and beverages purchased from said franchise. *SlangSite*

PTOMAINE TACO South of the border cuisine. *E.M. Vargas*

restaurant names
Abdominos, American Embassy, Anthrax, Black Anus, Booger's, Burger Thing, Choke 'n' Puke, Chunky Wheeze, Dead Slobster, Dingey's, El Pollo Cholo, El Torpedo, Fourbucks, Gag-in-the-Bag, Grubway, Hard Eats, I-SLOP, Mickey D's, Night Hassle, Pain for Us Café, Palais de Poulet, Rotten Ronnie's, Scary Cream, TGIFU, Taco Hell, Taco Smell, Tossin' Target, Das Wienerschitzel...

restaurant radius The number and variety of restaurants within convenient distance from work or home. *R. Stephens*

restaurant ratio [rule of thumb] The ratio of restaurants to population as a 'quality of life' index. (Also, 'eatertainment index') *I. Azimov*

RESUME Richly Exaggerated Saga of Utterly Meaningless Experience. *MAD*

retail elephant [See "big box"]

retro-traditional planning [See "neo-traditional planning"]

reurbanize When suburban-dwellers return to the city, either because their children have grown, they have recently separated or divorced, or perhaps have mowed one lawn too many. *F. Popcorn*

reutilization marketing yard Junkyard. *Federal Register*

RHYTHM Remember How You Treat Hazardous Materials. *Du Pont* [See "hasmat"]

right of way [ROW & R/W] 1) The right to get in the way. *W. Ballbach* 2) The Stephens' Law of Right of Way: [rule of thumb] The larger mass always has right of way— as true for navigation on the dance floor as on the ocean or highway. *R. Stephens*

riot renaissance architecture [See "architectural style"]

Ripperblade Slade Anti-environmentalist. The D-9 Caterpillar ripper blade removes all vegetation at ground level. *T. Slade* [See "environmentalist"]

road In the early days of the English language, *road* meant the act of riding, a journey upon a horse. The horseback journey itself was made upon a "highway," if upon the principal way between two cities, or upon a "way," if a lesser path were used. At that time *road* had a sinister meaning also. Because of the fact that a group of mounted men often betokened a hostile intent, *road* sometimes signified a foray by mounted men, an attach upon some person or district. The Scottish word *raid*, which Sir Walter Scott brought into English usage, is now often used to convey that meaning, and the old sense is still present in our word *inroad*. In reality *road* and *raid* are merely different spellings of the Old English *rad*, but the Scottish development went no further than the hostile foray. Through association of ideas, probably, the act of riding a horse was carried over to the act of riding the waves; hence, *road* also came to mean a place where ships may anchor with safety, a *roadstead*. This sense, wherein space and security were implied, seems to have affected the development of *road* into its present chief use, a public thoroughfare. Strangely enough this use which is now so common to us, was unknown much before the time of Shakespeare. *C. Funk*

Road Construction, Law of After large expenditures of federal, state, and county funds; after much confusion generated by detours and road blocks; after greatly annoying the surrounding population with noise, dust and fumes, the previously existing traffic jam is relocated by one-half mile. *A. Deitz*

road pizza [See "roadkill"]

road sign [See "signage"]

roadkill 1) Flattened fauna. ...animals that, like the Wicked Witch of the East in *The Wizard of Oz*, are not just merely dead but really most sincerely dead. *R. M. Knutson*

186

2) The proverbial pot-luck special at the local drive-in restaurant; a rare treat for anyone who has never tasted raccoon burgers or porcupine *cordon bleu*. *R. Bayan* [See "animals," "critter crossings" and "sailcat"]

Robin Hood Method [See "zone/zoning"]

robstacles Bollards used to prevent criminals from driving into stores to rob them. *E.M. Vargas* [See "bollards"]

Roll credits! End of presentation when speaker introduces project team or supporters. *R. Stephens*

rooftops Unit of urbanization measurement. Example "We won't get that 'costume cuisine' restaurant until we have more rooftops." *R. Stephens*

rotary [See "traffic circle"]

rough proportionality Government permit conditions and exactions constitute a taking unless the burden is roughly proportional to those impacts. The word 'rough' has dual meanings. *E.M. Vargas*

roundabout [See "traffic circle"]

rounding up the usual suspects [See "request for proposal"]

rubar The shoulder of the road, not paved. *N. French*

rubber chicken circuit, the Dinners organized by institutions. *R. Stephens*

rubbery ruler Inference that measurement is "elastic." *K. Sparks*

rules [See individual listing and "laws"]
AHWAHNEE PRINCIPLES
BUILDING GIANT RETAIL STORES
BUILDING HEIGHT
RULE OF FIVE
CARNIVAL PATTERN
COMMERCIAL PLANNING KILO-RULE
COMMUNITY OF 7,000 PATTERN
CONSULTING RULE
COUNTRY RUINATION RULE
DEMOCRACY BY DECIBEL
DEVELOPING REAL ESTATE
ENTERTAINMENT X TEN
ENVIRONMENTAL DOCS BY THE POUND
ENVIRONMENTAL ENFORCEMENT, BASIC RULE OF
GOD SQUAD PLANNING RULE OF THREE
GOLDEN RULE OF PLANNING
GOLF COURSE STANDARD
GRADE, MAXIMUM RECOMMENDED
GRANDMOTHER PRINCIPLE ON ETHICS
HOSPITAL SIZE
HOTEL RULE OF THREE
LAWYER-TO-LAWYER
LIQUOR LICENSE LIMIT
LOOKING AT HOUSES

Rule of Five, The [rule of thumb]

It seems that most city councils and planning commissions consist of the following five " characters":

THE READER: Reads everything, understands nothing. Usually a teacher or an accountant. (Comments often like: "On page 32, second paragraph, I believe you meant a colon and not a semi colon.   Also, on page 45, third line from the bottom, I believe it should read 'effect' and not 'affect'. Just some of my thoughts about the report and recommendations.")

THE SLEEPER: One of the highest attendance records. responds to

roll-call, "Here," but that may be the last sound from this member for the entire meeting.

THE STEPPING STONE: "Today the City Council, tomorrow the Board of Supervisors, then state senator, congressman. Maybe then Senator and, who knows, could be President. Happened before, why not me?"

THE DO-GOODER: Believes that government is here to help all of us. A believer in JFK's adage: Ask what you can do for your government (and, then, do it).

THE PARANOID: The opposite of the do-gooder. Believes he/she has to be in government or else they'll screw you.

F. Wein FAICP

rural country
ARCADIA An idealized rural locality known for its simple and quiet life. *P. Hellweg*
BFE [Bum F* Egypt] *Anon.*
BOONDOCKS An uninhabited area, esp. one overgrown with vegetation; any remote area, esp. in the countryside. *L. Urdang*
BOONIES *Anon.*
DUCKBURG Rural, provincial town. *Probert Encyclopaedia*
EAST CUPCAKE A very distant location out in the sticks, with the implication that it's not terribly civilized. Example: I've got to drive all the way to East Cupcake tomorrow to visit my in-laws. *SlangSite*
EAST PANCAKE Archetypal backwater. *J. Train*
HICK TOWN Where everybody knows whose check is good and whose wife isn't. *J. Adams*
LUBBOCK *Anon.*
PODUNK *Anon.*
SPRINGERSVILLE Another friendly name for our neighborhood trailerparks. *A. Williams*
SQUEEDUNK Small town. *Probert Encyclopaedia*
STICKS *Anon.*
TOOLIES *Anon.*
WHISTLE STOP Derogatory slang for a small, unimportant town. *Probert Encyclopaedia*

rural slammer [See "institutions"]

rural-urban transect A New Urbanism land use scale of six general types of environments:

1. Rural Preserve
2. Rural Reserve
3. Sub-Urban
4. General Urban
5. Urban Center
6. Urban Core

[See "New Urbanism"]

rurban Combining aspects of both rural and urban or suburban life. *E. Gargan*

S

S and M Surveying and Mapping. *D. Wood*

sagre [See "feste"]

sailcat [See "animals"]

saints [See "patron saints"]

salmon day The experience of spending an entire day swimming upstream only to get had and die in the end. *E. Williams*

sandbagged The condition of a water-bearing natural feature subject to emergency flood control measures including the filling of large burlap bags with sand to act as temporary levees. Or, the condition of an embarrassed planner who has just been publicly humiliated by an approval body for missing some key information in a staff report, without being given prior notice for preemptive action. *S. Matarazzo*

sanitary infill Politically-acceptable development or redevelopment of urban land that has been bypassed or underutilized. *R. Stephens*

satellite community/city [See "city"].

sausage home [See "house"]

saving place (saving face) Effort to preserve the dignity of a place. *R. Stephens*

-scape
BRANDSCAPE The brand landscape; the expanse of brands and brand-related items (logos, ads, and so on) within a culture or market. *R. Belk*
BUILTSCAPE A built scene. *UNCHS*
CITYSCAPE A panoramic or broad view of a large city, as *a cityscape of London*. *L. Urdang*
E-SCAPE Virtual reality scene. *R. Stephens*
ESCAPE To flee the scene. *R. Stephens*
ETHNOSCAPE A social scene. *UNCHS*
EUROSCAPE A European scene. *UNCHS*
GARAGESCAPE Subdivision in which narrow lots create views of garages only. *J. M. Fernandez AICP*
HARDSCAPE 1) A landscape consisting of man-made building materials such as asphalt, precast concrete, and the like, that developers feel customers perceive as forbidding. Hardscape especially refers to objects that are machinelike or machine-

made. *J. Garreau* 2) Doublespeak for concrete an asphalt. *Helping Our Peninsula's Environment*

LANDSCAPE 1) A natural scene. 2) Development requirement based on an area formula often without regard to urban design esthetics. E.g. The dead grass around the sign on the corner [obscene].

LIFESCAPE Depiction of life in any kind of art form or literature. *Parameswaran*

LIGHTSCAPE The total illumination or the pattern and distribution of lights in a picture or vista. *A. Kriegsman*

SEASCAPE A sea scene.

SOFTSCAPE Plants. Trees. The work of nature, as opposed to the work of man. *J. Garreau*

STREETSCAPE A road on which sufficient design review has been expended such that the street furniture, signage, and luminaires all match and/or are festooned with flags. *J. Garreau*

WATERSCAPE An aqueduct. *First American Title Company*

scents of place The odors, smells, aromas, and fragrances associated with a place. The most powerful of the senses is also the most overlooked in planning. *R. Stephens*

school planning rule of doubling [rule of thumb] School requirements double at each level of education. *R. Stephens*

- ELEMENTARY SCHOOL 12-acre school per 600 students or 1,200 homes
- MIDDLE SCHOOL: 25-acre school per 1,200 students or 2,400 homes.
- HIGH SCHOOL: 50-acre school per 2,400 students or 4,800 homes.
- JUNIOR COLLEGE: 100-acre school per 4,800 students or 9,600 homes.
- COLLEGE: 200-acre school per 9,600 students or 19,200 homes.
- UNIVERSITY: 400-acre school per 19,200 students or 38,400 homes.

schwoogie A road with many curves. *SlangSite*

scientific resources [See "resources"]

SCRUB Special City Regulation of Unsavory Businesses. An ordinance to restrict or prohibit offensive businesses. *R. Stephens* [See "ZOT!]

Seagull Management Style "Fly in, crap all over desk, walk out." *P. Bedford*

seagull manager A manager who flies in, makes a lot of noise, dumps all over everything and then leaves.

seasononium [See "condominia"]

seat cushion [See public hearing/meeting participants]

second street Average, lackluster or normal. Stemming from the fact that Second Street is the most common street name in the United States. *Pseudodictionary*

seeing the light Switching from public sector to private sector. *K. Laufenburger* {See "gone native" and "turning to the dark side"]

seismic event Earthquake. *W. Lutz*

seismically designed high rise In an earthquake, the structure will not collapse, but will drop all of its glass and stone panels into the street turning pedestrians into a stew-like mush of pureed flesh. *Glass Steel and Stone*

semi-detached Sharing a party wall. *R. Holder*

senior congregate living community for the chronologically gifted Retirement community. *W. Lutz* [See "NORC" and "raisin ranch"]

sense of community The relationships of the people within a place.

sense of entry The front door is big and far away. *Glass Steel and Stone*

sense of immunity Mistaken belief that land use regulation does not apply for a particular neighborhood or site. *R. Stephens*

sense of place The characteristics of a location that make it readily recognizable as being unique and different from its surroundings. *M. Schultz*

setback 1) The distance between the street right-of-way line and the front line of a building or any projection thereof, excluding uncovered steps. 2) Prominent condition in development process. *R. Stephens*

Seven Dwarfs Test, The [rule of thumb] Interview test to determine applicant's achievement capabilities: "Name the Seven Dwarfs." The more dwarfs correctly named, the lower achievement anticipated. Planners unable to name a single dwarf are suitable for upper management. *K. Downs* [The "politically correct" name for this test is The Seven Vertically Challenged Exam *R. Stephens*] Near misses: Bilbo, Billy Barty, Cheesy, Chubby, Chunky, Curly, Droopy, Dumpy, Flakey, Hoppy, Lumpy, Messy, Mopey, Pee Wee, Porky, Shorty, Slap Happy, Sleazy, Sloppy, Smiley, Snorty, Snoozy, Tatoo, Wheezy, Wimpy, Zeppo.

sewergator [See "animals"]

shake 'n' bake Earthquake followed by fire. *R. Stephens*

shamboozle To acquire a liquor license permit by elaborate methods of deceit. *Anon.*

shame train The bus. *J. Price*

shelfware The bound, printed version of a project, which likely will end up on a shelf, unused and forgotten, gathering dust. *Pseudodictionary*

shopping mall 1) Shopping maul. Suburban madness. *H Eng AICP* 2) The marketplace that killed Main Street; a synthetic conglomeration of shops and teenagers reproduced along more or less identical lines throughout the North American continent, so that intelligent visitors may experience the same chill of alienation wherever their travels take them. *R. Bayan* [See "podmall"]

shot of planicillin Planning to prevent SOB's. *E.M. Vargas* [See "SOB" and "ZOTs"]

sick building Structure with self-generated, internal air pollution. [See "BRI," "housitosis" and "Smart Building"] *R. Stephens*

sidewalk clutter Street furniture and street hardware that is not in the street, but on the sidewalk. Example: "With all the tree grids, hydrants, lighting standards, signs, and other sidewalk clutter, we could barely walk side-by-side." *J. Stephens* [See "street furniture"]

sightsee-sick The "Yes, old building, ancient...where do you get an ice cream in this

197

place?" feeling when you've visited 20 monuments in 3 days. *Pseudodictionary* [See "Monumentenmoe"]

signage 1) Signs. Especially those which are products of the expenditure of vastly more money on design review than would seem plausible, given the appearance and function of the result, which is to announce "No Left Turn" and the like. Etymology: The guardians of urban esthetics have for decades decried the proliferation of shopping center beacons that makes each nonlimited-access highway resemble the Las Vegas Strip. Thus, developers of large tracks of land who aspire to the label "megadeveloper" indicate their seriousness of purpose, attention to detail, and desire for social acceptance by hiring designers to create signs of a style that are not merely informative, but are distinct to the development. Hence, signage— probably a contraction of 'signs' and 'signature.' *J. Garreau* 2) Sign plannage, or possibly a contraction of 'signs' and 'garbage.'. *R. Stephens*
ADVERTECTURE Advertisements painted on the walls of buildings. *R. Salutin* [See "duck"]
ANGRY FRUIT SALAD Sign that uses too many colors. *Anon.*
BANDIT SIGN An illegal commercial sign posted in a public area. *J. Catalano*
GHOST SIGN The remnant of a vintage advertisement painted on the side of a building.
GROUND-MOUNTED CONFIRMATORY ROUTE MARKERS. Road sign. *W. Lutz*
JAWS Jumbo Abrasive Wall Signs. *Anon.*
LITTER ON A STICK Billboards. *Anon.*
LOGO BUILDING Trademark building designed to attract motorists. *Anon.*
REASSURANCE SIGN When trying to locate an attraction, especially when the route is long and unclear, it is critical to offer "reassurance signs" that tell the visitor they are indeed going the right way. *Southeast Tourism Society*
ROTATING SIGN "Here's your 360-degree architecture!"

STOPTIONAL A stop sign in the middle of nowhere. *Pseudodictionary*

STREET SPAM Advertisements posted on telephone poles, traffic lights, and other public areas. *B. Snyder*

TODS Tourist Oriented Directional Signage. *Southeast Tourism Society*

TRADE DRESS Colors or logo style that become associated with a product or company. *K. Watts*

VERTICAL LITTER [See "signage, street spam"]

WAYFINDING SIGNAGE Signs to aid the public in orienting themselves geographically within a specific location and which identify functional units within the location. *Southeast Tourism Society*

signage letter size [rule of thumb] When designing messages to be read from moving vehicles, type must be larger—3" high at 100' and at least 12" high at 400'. Messages must be very simple—no more than one picture and less than seven words. *W. Kaufmann*

signature building 1) You can't afford it. *Glass Steel and Stone* [See "billboard building"]

silent city Cemetery. *J. Green*

silver bullet Simple solution. From the folktale ability of a silver bullet to kill a werewolf. *L. Dalton PhD AICP*

Sinatra [See "public hearing/meeting participants"]

sindrome A place of public sexual performance. *S. Berliner* [See "SOB"]

199

single-family home [See "house"]

sink screening The process of renaming, hiding and disguising 'sinks.' *G. Clay* [See "sinks"]

sinks Places of last resort into which powerful groups in society shunt, shove, dump, and pour whatever or whomever they do not like or cannot use: auto carcasses, garbage, trash, and minority groups. *G. Clay*

sit down, shut up, buckle down, and bang on Call to order at a volatile hearing/meeting. *R. Stephens*

sitting on prime time Prime commercial location. (television) *G. Clay*

situation A problem of unimaginable, much less soluble, proportions. *J. Garreau*

situs Location; setting; usually refers to the economic merits of the area in which a property is located. Example: "The house would be worth $30,000 anywhere else. But in that situs—a little block of brownstones—it should bring at least $75,000." *D.E. Miller*

size of Wales Imperial measurement of area. Used to convey bigness of ecological damage etc. (British) *Pseudodictionary* [See "sports analogies"]

skewed grid The design looked too boring with a regular grid. *Glass Steel and Stone*

skyclutter All the things that obstruct a view of the sky including signs, poles, wires, etc. Fortunately, we have attenuated to this pollution and do not 'see' them. *R.*

Stephens

SLAPP Strategic Lawsuit Against Public Participation. *G. Pring*

sleeping policeman Speed bump. It might be more accurate to refer to as a sleeping *traffic engineer*. *C. Chipping* [See "street calming"]

SLOAP Space Left Over After Planning. *M. Kahn*

slope analysis Map that shows areas of varying slope by grade. *Anon.*

slope expression The grade, ratio or angle of the land describing how flat or steep it is. For example a 100% grade is a 1:1 ratio and a 45 degree angle. *R. Stephens*

sloppy copy A draft of a document that lacks neatness, correct spelling, grammar, and structure. *I. Faynik*

slow motion replay [See "public hearing/meeting"]

Slums and Bums Urban sociology college courses. *J. Green*

smart Plannerese for 'planned' or 'high tech." *R. Stephens*
SMART BALM (smart bomb) Using the word "smart" as a modifier for rational or hi-tech planning. *R. Stephens*
SMART BUILDING   Structure with automated monitoring and regulation of infrastructure. Smart buildings are often the ones with air-conditioning on during rainy weather, the heater on during broiling weather; and no opening windows. The resulting building chills, fever and poor ventilation sometimes create a "sick [smart]

building ". *R. Stephens*

SMART COMMUNITY A community integrated with information technology and communications (ITC). Typically with an intranet. *R. Stephens*

SMART DEVELOPMENT Modern development adhering to 6 principles:

SMART GROWTH An urban planning philosophy which isn't about battling growth, but managing it sensibly and progressively. It was adopted early on by Maryland Gov. Paris Glendenning to "steer the state's infrastructure dollars…to discourage sprawl and encourage development or redevelopment in already settled communities." *F. Popcorn*

SMART STREETS A planning scheme for new towns where technology such as fiber optics is built into the infrastructure just like water, sewer and storm drains. *B. Inman*

SME Subject Matter Expert *T. Hardin*

smokescreened Frequent occurrence in development review process where one issue [usually minor] takes all the time and important issues are left unresolved. *M. Roos AICP*

sniffers [See "environmentalist"]

snout house [See "house"]

SOB Sexually Oriented Business. *K. Gutierrez AICP*

SOB Curve "Slide Over, Baby" …said the driver to the passenger on the sharp right curve. Street curves which have small radii relative to their design speed. *C. Herron*

social engineering Planning. (Japan) *Y. Kumata*

202

social landmark   Neighborhood institution that serves as a community gathering place. *J. Gath*

soft costs   The fees charged to obtain the services of architects, government registrars, [planners] and the like. The costs of whatever goes into a building that does not represent a tangible object such as a brick. The location where developers have the highest danger of losing their shirts. *J. Garreau*

soft report   A technical report which is less critical of a project. *R. Greenwood*

solid exhaust emission   Manure. *S. Steel*

some assemblage required   The necessary acquisition of contiguous properties into one ownership for a specific use. *R. Stephens*

sourpoint presentation   PowerPoint slides showing how bad a place is to solicit support for development. *R. Stephens*

Soylent Green   [See "green"]

spaghetti bowl   Complex curvilinear street system as opposed to the grid system. *R. Masyczek* [See "Dead Worm Syndrome" and "loops and lollipops"]

SPARK   School/PARKs program. *City of Houston*

speaking in tongues   Complex presentation in Plannerese or technical jargon. [Unintelligible speech generally uttered in a dissociated or trance state.] *R. Stephens*

[See "glossolalia"]

Special Interest Group (SIG) Politically organized liberals. *T. Sowell*

Special Interest Lobby Politically organized conservatives. *T. Sowell* Also ' gucci gulch.'

special interests
ASTROTURF Pseudo-grassroots.
BIRDS 'N' BUNNIES Environmental lobby
GOD SQUAD Religious group.
GRASSROOTS Ordinary people.
GREAT UNWASHED Ordinary people.
GUCCI GULCH Lobbyists
PAC Political action committee
PLU People like us

Species Area Law The smaller the habitat, the fewer species the habitat will support. *Helping Our Peninsula's Environment*

speed hump A more 'driver-friendly' speed bump. ('Speed Hump' warning signs are collector items for teens) *R. Stephens* [See "street calming"]

spinach [See "architectural ornamentation"]

spite fence A fence built for the purpose of causing a problem for one's neighbor. May ruin the view, make access of a vehicle difficult, etc., or simply be ugly. *First American Title Co.*

splace Of or referring to a parking place or space. Example: "It was hard for me to find a parking splace when I went to the mall on Friday." *SlangSite* [See "parking"]

sports analogies [rules of thumb] Analogies to sports to help decision-makers and the public visualize typical planning measurements. *R. Stephens*
BASEBALL ANALOGY Liking smart growth or new urbanism, but not liking higher density is the same as liking the sport of baseball, but not liking bats. Without them, you simply can't play. *R. Stephens*
BASKETBALL ANALOGY A cubic foot is about the size of a basketball. For example, a small stream flowing at twenty cubic feet per second (20 cfs) is equivalent in volume to 20 basketballs per second.
BASKETBALL COURT ANALOGY A 5,000-square-foot lot or building is about the same area as a 50x94-foot basketball court. ['The Suburbs' is basketball slang for a long distance from the basket.]
FBLS Abbreviation of football fields when used as a unit of measure. 1 fbl. equals approximately 100 yards. Used by media outlets and the Discovery channel to describe objects of arbitrary 'biggness' to audiences who, evidently, are unable to relate size to anything but football. Example: "The moon is over 3 billion feet from the earth. That's over 10 million fbls." *SlangSite*
FOOTBALL FIELD ANALOGY 1) An acre is approximately (91%) the size of a 160x300-foot football field (no end zones). For example, a championship golf course can be compared to the size of 180 football fields. 2) An acre-foot of water is approximately the amount of water to cover a football field one foot deep. 3 acre-feet is about a football field with 3 feet of water or 1,000,000 gallons.
SWIMMING POOL ANALOGY   An 11,000-square-foot lot or building is approximately the size of a collegiate racing pool (11,250sf). A 13,000-square-foot lot or building is approximately the area of an Olympic racing pool (25x50m).

TENNIS COURT ANALOGY The standard suburban 7,200-square-foot lot is the same area as a 60x120 foot tennis court. [See "subdivision efficiency" and "suburban subdivision standard"]

VOLLEYBALL COURT ANALOGY A 4,000-square-foot lot or building is the same area as a 50x80-foot volleyball court.

[See "imperial system of measurement," "Plan your dive" and "regulations"]

sprawl Haphazard growth or extension outward, especially that resulting from real estate development on the outskirts of a city: *urban sprawl.* Also, "urban scatterization." [See "suburbia" and "weapon of mass construction"]

SPRAWL BRAWL *F. Popcorn*

SPRAWL OUT Describes unchecked suburban growth, also called the 'sprawl brawl.' *F. Popcorn*

SPRAWL OVERHAUL Redevelopment district. *R. Stephens*

TELESPRAWL An unintended consequence of telecommuting. Freed from the daily grind, office-liberated workers relocate beyond typical commuting range, creating new kinds of environmental stresses and strains in formerly rural neighborhoods. When Agways are replaced by Starbucks, blame telesprawl. *F. Popcorn*

squatter settlements A settlement, lacking services, which consists of a collection of small, crude shacks made of discarded materials and serving as habitation for poor people on the outskirts of towns, especially in South America and Africa. *Parole*

BARRIADES Squatter settlement. (Peruvian)

FAVELAS Slum settlement or shanty town. (Brazilian)

KATCHI ABADI Squatter camp. (Indian)

POBLACION Squatter settlement. (Chilean)

RANCHERIAS Squatter settlement. (Mexican)

SHANTY TOWN Squatter settlement.

TOWNSHIP 1 In the former Republic of South Africa, separate areas of geneally low standard housing reserved for Africans, Asians or 'coloured' people.

squeedunk [See "rural country"]

squirrel leather The "tanned" remains of a squirrel which has been repeatedly run over on the street and baked in the sun; also applies to other roadkill: "bunny leather," "raccoon leather," "bird leather," etc. *Pseudodictionary* [See "roadkill"]

squatter's field Land 'settled' on by neighbors without the permission of the owner. *E.M. Vargas* [See "land donor" and "trespass"]

squish test If it "squishes" when you walk on it, it's "wetlands". *R. Schonholtz* [See "wetlands"]

stacking distance [rule of thumb] 1) Use twenty feet (20') per car to estimate the length of cars waiting at an intersection or lined up at a drive-thru. I.e. 100' will accommodate five cars. 2) Use 2 feet per (2') person to estimate the number of people lined up at the counter or podium. I.e. 30' will accommodate fifteen people. *R. Stephens*

stacks Raw materials concentrated into local heaps, piles, or tanks. *G. Clay*

stall A barn or parking space. A clear example of the U.S. connection between horse and car. (Horse thieves were lynched, murderers were tried). *R. Stephens*

starter castle [See "mansionization"]

starter home [See "house"]

Stay Free Mini-Pad A homeless shelter for very short people. *R. M. Robinson AICP*

Stephens' Law of Right of Way [See "right of way"]

sticks and bricks (Stick-built) The materials with which Residential is usually built, as opposed to the steel and concrete of Commercial. *J. Garreau*

stippling Adding small, dark dots to open spaces on a map or plan to add visual interest and contrast. (cartography) *A. Davies*

stones and bones Prehistoric cultural resources. [See "artichokes" and "resources"] *R. Stephens*

Stop 'n' Rob All-night convenience store. *M. Brodeur*

store-to-area ratio [rule of thumb] In master-planned communities, about 5-10% of the total area will support and suffice for commercial uses. *R. Stephens* [See "commercial planning kilo-law" and "F.A.R."]

stories The floors of buildings are called stories because early European builders used to paint picture stories on the sides of their houses. Each floor had a different story. (In Europe, the '1st floor' is the 'ground floor' and the 2nd floor is the 1st story) *Real Estate Humor*

Storybook Style [See "architectural style"]

strategery After being coined by Saturday Night Live writers to poke fun at George Bush, one group of presidential advisors with a sense of humor named themselves "The Strategery Group." Now it seems every talking head on TV uses "strategery" without realizing there's no such word. *W. Smith*

strategic planning Planning warfare. *W. Wasels*

street calming Efforts to minimize traffic impacts to residential and commercial neighborhoods. This program reduces the "thrill-seeking" aspect of being a pedestrian. One technique involves elongated [14-20'] speed bumps. These are not referred to as speed *humps* because 1) many activists don't want to include the expression in their working vocabulary, and 2) an increase in theft could be anticipated from signs reading "Speed Hump Ahead". *S. Hartnett* [See "sleeping policeman" and "speed hump"]

street coverage [rule of thumb] ~20% of any large project total area will be used for streets and vehicle access. *R. Stephens*

street design [rule of thumb] A city street is most visually appealing if its width is the same as the height of the buildings along it. *D. Russell*

street furniture Everything exposed to the weather put there by the hand of man, not counting roads, buildings, and plants. This "everything else" is far more considerable than most people recognize, because it is usually so plain or so ugly—and thus ignored as a feature of the landscape—as to render it virtually invisible. It includes newspaper vending boxes, stoplights, no-parking signs, and those circular iron grills sometimes put around the bases of trees when they are embedded in a sidewalk. Not to mention, of course, furniture. Like benches. *J. Garreau* [See "sidewalk clutter"]

209

street muzak Street sounds such as traffic and people talking played as background in artificial 'downtown' environments. Example: "We were at DisneyWalk last evening and found a speaker in a fake rock. Street muzak was just barely audible." *R. Stephens*

street people
BEN HUR Shopping cart charioteer. *J. Stephens*
BUS BENCH PHILOSOPHER Neurotic. *C. Bright*
CHARIOT RACE Multiple shopping carts. *J. Stephens*
COGNITIVELY DISADVANTAGED PARAURBAN INHABITANTS. Politically correct terminology. *R. Stephens*
FLOATER An undesirable. *R. Holder*
GENTLEMAN OF THE ROAD (British and New Zealand) *Probert Encyclopaedia*
GUTTER PUNK A modern young hobo traveler usually sporting a backpack, dreaded hair, and patches. *PseudoDictionary*
NEW AGE TRAVELLERS Vagrants (British) *R. Holder*
PAVEMENT PEOPLE Homeless beggars. *R. Holder*
PERFORMANCE ARTIST A street loonie with a foundation grant. *R. Bayan*
ROSE PARADE Multiple 'shopping cart cruisers.' *R. Stephens*
SELF-EMPLOYED OUTDOOR MONETARY SOLICITOR. Politically Correct Terminology. *R. Bayan*
SHOPPING CART CRUISER Miniature parade float made from 'borrowed' shopping cart. *R. Stephens*
SIDEWALK PSYCHOTIC *Anon.*
SIDEWALK SALE The collection of people hanging outside a club after it closes, hoping to get a date to finish off their evening. Example: "There was this cute guy there at the sidewalk sale, but someone else walked up to him before I got up my

nerve." *SlangSite*
SIDEWALK SOLILOQUISTS Street persons who talk to themselves. *R. Stephens*
SIDEWALK SURFER Skateboarder. *Anon.*
STREET LOONIES Generally the only big-city inhabitants a stranger may count on for honest conversation. *R. Bayan*
STREET PERFORMER Artist whose stage is the sidewalk. Also, 'performance artist.'
URBAN OUTDOORSMAN *E. Adkison*

strike An effort to increase egg production by strangling the chicken. *Nevada Nut & Bolt, Inc.*

stringer Contract planner. (From newspaper term for freelancers employed for special reports) *J. Proust* [See "technical assistant"]

strip commercial Adult entertainment use. J. Marquez [See "SOB"]

strip mining [See "environmental art"]

studentia An overabundance of students who take over an area usually populated by good folk. On the order of *rodentia*. *SlangSite* [See "studentification" and "town/gown split"]

studentification The changes caused by a large number of students moving into a neighborhood or community, particularly university students attending a nearby school. *A. Blythe* [See "studentia" and "town/gown split"]

substandard housing Slum *P. Dickson*

subdivision   The division of a tract of land into defined lots for single-family detached residential development.

COOKIE CUTTER SUBDIVISION   Vanilla subdivision in which all lots are uniform in size. *Anon.*

COUNTRYCLUBDIVISION   Upscale with a country club.

GOLFCLUBDIVISION   Golf-oriented

SHLUBDIVISION   Out-of-date or poorly designed

SHRUBDIVISION   Park-oriented

SNUBDIVISION   Upscale with attitude

YACHTCLUBDIVISION   Boating-oriented

Subdivision Cost Rule of Five [rule of thumb] A rule of thumb used to estimate subdivision costs. Basically, 1/5 of the sales price pertains to land, 1/5 to improvements, 2/5 to administration, and 1/5 to miscellaneous costs. *Kenneth Leventhal & Company*

subdivision efficiency [rule of thumb] Narrower lots are more efficient than shallower lots as less infrastructure (street and utility line) is required per unit. Practical efficiency is reached at about 1:2 width to depth ratio. For example 60x120 feet for a standard suburban subdivision lot. *R. Stephens* [See "suburban subdivision standard," "tennis court analogy" and "tetris tract"]

subdivision scale [rule of thumb] The following scale is from smallest to largest. *K. Downs & R.. Stephens* [See "lot"]

1.   ZERO LOT   A lot moving towards 0 square feet. The smallest unit of single-family detached residential defined by the width of a garage.

2.   COTTAGE OR GARDEN LOT   Anything smaller than a standard lot that still has vegetation. [See "house"]

3. STANDARD LOT The 7,200 square foot; 72 feet wide by 100 feet deep. The standard subdivision building block. [See "suburban subdivision standard"]
4. ESTATE Anything larger than a standard lot. [See "estate"]
5. VILLA The last urban development prior to allusions of farm-life.
6. RANCHITO Smaller than a farmette or ranchette, but with some agricultural character.
7. FARMETTE More land than is logical to mow but not enough to plow. *J. Garreau* [See "corporate campus"]
8. RANCHETTE A single dwelling unit occupied by a non-farming household on a parcel of 2.5 to 20 acres that has been subdivided from agricultural land. *California Planning Roundtable*
9. FARM A large subdivision or community. [See "patroonship"]
10. RANCH, RANCHO A very large community or even city that may no longer include any ranching activities.

subliminage/sublimagery Subliminal image/imagery. Example: "The dead-end street on that tract map had a distinct phallic subliminage." *E.M. Vargas*

suburb (international)

FRENCH	banlieue / faubourg
GERMAN	Vorort
ITALIAN	quartiere periferico
SPANISH	periferia

suburban drool The continuous, low-flow drainage from development. i.e. runoff from watering the lawn and washing the car. *R. Emerson*

suburban subdivision standard [rule of thumb] The gross density for a subdivision

213

with 7,200-square-foot lots averages four units per acre (4 DU/Ac). When attrition due to design constraints and exactions is factored, it is closer to three and one-half units per acre (3.5 DU/Ac). In some jurisdictions, this is the fine line between 'rural country estates' and 'future urban slums.' *R. Stephens* [See "density," "exactions," "quality of life formula," "street coverage," and "subdivision scale"]

suburban trips per day [rule of thumb] The average suburban household generates ten (10) vehicle trips per day. *J. Kain AICP*

suburbarian Primitive suburban dweller. *R. Stephens*

suburbia
1) Suburbia is where the developer bulldozes out the trees, then names the streets after them. *B. Vaughn* 2) A scattered archipelago of residential enclaves offering neither the diversions of city life nor the rustic solace of the countryside; a world characterized by a comforting blandness of architecture and mental outlook, which may explain why it has lured a statistical majority of the American populace. *R. Bayan* 3) That boring hell where all the houses are identical in size and shape. *SlangSite* 4) A womb with a view. *J. Clapp* 5) There's no there, there. *G. Stein*
BACK BLOCKS Outer suburbs, beyond the city [Australian]. *Probert Encyclopedia*
BADDABOOMBURB Rustbelt boomburb. *E.M. Vargas* [See "belts"]
BARRIO A suburb (Spanish). *H.F. Byrne* [See "suburb (international)"]
BETTY CROCKER SUBURB Suburb without child care facilities— "mom stays home with the kids." *Anon.*
BIZ BURBS [Business Suburbs] Former bedroom communities that have been transformed to job centers through massive commercial development. Once suburbs, they are now industrialized and are also referred to as Edge Cities. *B. Inman*
BLURB Indistinguishable suburban neighborhoods. *R. Stephens*

BOOMBURB   An area that currently has more than 100,000 residents and has maintained double-digit rates of population growth in each recent decade, but is not the largest city in its metropolitan area. Boomburbs almost never have a dense central business area. And their housing, retail, entertainment, and offices are spread out and loosely configured. *Fannie Mae Foundation*

BOOMTOWN   Town characterized by explosive growth. *Parole*

BURBCLAVE   Burb + [en]clave. A self-contained and like-minded community, usually catering to a specific class or race. *Parole*

THE BURBS   Suburbs. *Anon.*

CHILD-CENTERED COMMUNITY   Child-centered communities where everyone is an amateur psychologist or sociologist. *J. Clapp*

CONURBATION   *L. Mumford*

DECENTRALIZATION   The movement of people and businesses from a central area (a city or downtown area) to more scattered positions (surrounding suburbs). *Real Estate Dictionary*

EXURBIA   the indistinct expansion of the city beyond its limits. The landscape out of the city, composed from heterogenic elements overlapped amongst themselves residential areas, agricultural terrain, big containers. *P. Roth*

sprinkler city   A fast-growing outer suburb or exurb. *D. Lease*

FAUXBURB   Modern suburb replicating post-WWII suburbs with eclectic (non-themed) architecture. *R. Stephens*

MALLBURBIA   The business community that has developed in the vicinity of a mall. Example: "After shopping at the mall my sister and I had more things to pick-up and we found them in mallburbia." *SlangSite*

PENTURBAN   Relating to the residential area or community beyond a city's suburbs. *J. Lessinger*

PETER PAN SUBURB   Suburb designed without consideration for the elderly— the residents "never grow old." *L. Keppelman*

THE RHUBARBS The suburbs. *Probert Encyclopaedia*

SHRUBURBS   That point just outside the city where it seems each homeowner is competing in the nicest trimmed hedge contest. Example: "The shruburbs are a refreshing contrast to the concrete jungle of the inner city." *SlangSite*

SITCOM SUBURB Neighborhoods of traditional Cape Cod or colonial houses with neat front lawns. *D. Hayden*

SORORITY HOME COMMUNITY Sorority home communities with kids. *J. Clapp*

SPRINKLER CITY A fast-growing outer suburb or exurb. *D. Brooks*

STUBURBIA A part of a metropolis that resembles a suburb. Known as gentrification it usually results in one or more Starbuck's. *J. Tuberville*

SUBURBIDITY (turbidity) A thick, hazy condition of sense of place. *R. Stephens*

TECHNOBURB An exurb with decentralized, city-quality infrastructure, industries, and services; an exurb that contains a disproportionate number of technology-based businesses. *R. Fishman*

TRANSNATIONAL SUBURB   A suburb made up mostly of immigrants who maintain strong ties to their home countries. *J. Chang*

VAVAVOOMBURB A boomburb with pizzazz. *R. Stephens*

ZOOMBURB A place growing even faster than a boomburb. *D. Hayden*

[See "edge city"]

suits [See "public hearing/meeting participants"]

sunshine law violation Decision-making made where the sun don't shine. *E.M. Vargas*

supercommuter A person whose round trip to work exceeds a hundred miles each day. *J. Garreau*

supermarket The grocery store that made grocers obsolete. A prodigious pantry stocked with enough varieties of breakfast cereal to cause acute nervous disorders in sensitive shoppers, esp. those lately arrived from Third World nations. *R. Bayan* [See "hypermarket"]

surreal estate Properties with an oddly dreamlike quality. *R. Stephens* [See "real estate"]

Survey says! The moment when the vote appears on the council chambers electronic voting board. From the TV show 'Family Feud.' *R. Stephens*

survival syndrome [See "agency anorexia"]

sustainable development 1) The in-word of the nineties, meaning the opposite of built-in obsolescence. *E. Poventud* 2) Development started and kept going by planners who see no end in sight. *W. Wasels*

SWAG Slightly [Sophisticated, Scientific] Wild-Assed Guess. *Anon.*

swap meat/meet Night club or bar. Not to be confused with a *swap meet*. *E.M. Vargas*

swarming The coming together by impulse-determination of mobile communities. I.e. Woodstock. *G. Clay*

swimming pool rule [rule of thumb] 450 square feet of water surface for each 1,000 persons (15sf ws/3% pop). A 25-yard pool serves 10,000 people. The average 50-meter pool [~9,000sf] serves about 20,000 people. *J. DeChiara* [See "natatorium"]

swimming pool analogy [See "sports analogies"]

Swipple Rule of Order [See "democracy by decibel" and "rules of thumb"]

SWOT Strengths, Weaknesses, Opportunities, Threats. A community analysis. *P. Wilkinson*

symposium Greeks of old did not customarily drink with their meals. Instead, after a dinner was finished, the host and his guests—and perhaps some guests who had not attended the dinner—were served wine to the extent that might be desired. This drinking party was called *symposion* (taken into Latin as *symposium*), derived from *syn*, together, and *poton*, drink. These occasions, enjoyed by men only, were accompanied by music, dancing, games, or other amusements, or sometimes merely by agreeable conversation. It is through the latter diversion that, nowadays, we regard a *symposium* as a discussion by several persons upon a given topic, often in writing. But drink, although the essence of the original word, is no longer necessarily an accompanying feature. *C. Funk*

T

table stable A cube farm without the cubes. i.e. a room full of tables, one for each employee. Example: "Do your programmers live in a cube farm or a table stable?" *SlangSite* [See "cube farm"]

tagger 1) Graffiti practitioner. 2) Visual terrorist. [See "graffiti"] 3) Piecer. Person whose graffiti aspires for higher aesthetics. [See "urban guerrilla artist"]

talkin' talents Oratory skills. (cowboy) *R. Adams*

Tara Property subject to hurricanes, storms, Santa Ana Winds, chinooks, or tornadoes. (Gone with the Wind) *R. Stephens*

TARD The American Residential Dream. The suburban building block. *J. Stephens*
- Single-family detached house
- Bedroom for each family member
- Multiple-car/adult toy garage
- Front yard lawn
- Back yard barbecue/pool
- Side yard dog run/garden
- 6-foot side- and backyard wood fence
- front yard picket fence optional

Tarzan Ethics Evolving environmental ethics parallel the depiction of Tarzan in popular media. The original films show Tarzan killing virtually every animal he meets. Decade after decade the media have shifted according to prevalent ethical standards. Currently, Tarzan is shown as a simpleton who must be guided by the wiser animal community. *R. Stephens* [See "green"]

Taupeville A neighborhood that requires buildings to be all neutral colors, usually beige and taupe. Generic, non-descript, lacking in personality and boring. Example: "We're much too eclectic to live in Taupeville. 'Over the taupe' implies something more creative or excessive." *Pseudodictionary* [See "earth tones" and "suburbia"]

tavern [See "pavilion"]

tchotchkeria   A place that sells tchotchkes. From Yiddish "tchotchke," meaning useless little object (knicknack), and Spanish "taqueria," meaning a restaurant that specializes in tacos and other Mexican fast food. Usually found in "quaint" towns, usually patronized almost exclusively by middle-class females of all ages, usually exuding a stench of potpourri all the way out to the sidewalk. Variations: "New Age tchotchkeria," a place which sells candles, incense, statues of goddesses, meditation cushions, etc.; and "upscale tchotchekeria," where you can buy Waterford crystal collectibles, Lladro figurines, and the like. The towns of New England are simply rife with tchotchkerias. *Pseudodictionary*

tear factor   The unknown effect of crying at a public hearing or meeting.   *R. Stephens*

teardown [See "mansionization"]

technical assistant   Euphemism for municipal contract planner. [See "stringer"]

technical projects rule of two   [rule of thumb] Complex technical projects always take twice as long to finish as your most thorough and conservative estimate, even when you've used this rule and doubled your first estimate.   *R. Cumberford*

technology impact studies   It's hard to imagine, but there was a time before Environmental Studies existed as a discipline. Technology Impact Studies—which hasn't yet emerged as an academic field—will have a similar trajectory. This multi-disciplinary area will examine the impact of technology on our lives and our culture—both positive and negative (the latter will be given the moniker 'wrecknowledge"). *F. Popcorn*

Teflon Planning [See "velcro planning"]   The adoption of a plan, after which time every important decision is made without reference to such plan. *P. Sedway AICP*

telecom hotel [See "telecommunications"]

telecommuting Using telecommunications to work from home or other locations instead of at the organization's premises.

teleophobia Fear of definite plans. *B. Clark*

telecommunications
BIRD Telecommunications satellite.
CELLULAR CELLAR Underground vault for cell tower equipment.
IT&T I telephoned and tagged.
PROGRAM [See "program"]
TEL/COM or TELECON Telephone communication [more impressive than a phone call?].
TELECOM HOTEL A building designed to hold only telecommunications equipment. *J. Holusha*
TELECONFERENCE More than 2 people on the phone at the same time.
TELEPHONE TAG and TELEPHONE PING PONG Unsuccessful attempts to return each other's phone call.
TELESPRAWL [See "sprawl"]

Ten Commandments of Negotiating Development
I Thou shalt negotiate in good faith and sincerity and try to meet thy opposite party's "bottom line."
II Thou shalt not skin thy opposite party when a sandpapering is enough to achieve thy objective.

III Thou shalt do thy homework, organize and anticipate issues in thy negotiations.

IV Thou shalt remember thou are not dealing across the table with creatures of logic—but of emotions—bristling with prejudices, motivated by pride and vanity.

V If thou intend to ask for something, thou shalt ask for it early in the negotiations.

VI Thou shalt say "no" on an issue at the beginning if thou can't say anything else, and thou shalt not ask for that which thee already has.

VII Thou shalt not become angry, red of face, or loud of voice unless it is intentional on thy part.

VIII Thou shalt know thy limits and go no further. Thou shalt have "deal makers" at the table whenever possible.

IX Thou shalt observe the attorney-to-attorney respect rule.

X Thou shalt know thine own "bottom line" and shalt keep thy negotiating package intact.

W. H. Claire III AICP

Ten Principles We Can Build Upon *Prince Charles*

1. The Place – Don't rape the landscape
2. Hierarchy – If a building can't express itself, how can we understand it?
3. Scale – Less might be more; too much is not enough
4. Harmony – Sing with the choir and not against it
5. Enclosure – Give us somewhere safe for the children to play and let the wind play somewhere else
6. Materials – Let where it is be what it's made of
7. Decoration – A bare outline won't do; give us the details
8. Art – Michelangelo accepted very few commissions for a free-standing abstract sculpture in the forecourt [See "plunk art"]
9. Signs & Lights – Don't make rude signs in public places
10. Community – Let the people who will have to live with what you build help

guide your hand

tenement [See "walk-up"]

tennis court analogy [See "sports analogies"]

tentative map A not fully worked out, concluded, or agreed on; provisional map. *Anon.*

TEO Strategy Total Environmental Opportunities. The ultimate economically smart strategy for companies for waste reduction, waste minimization, source reduction, and pollution prevention— terms which generally cover the spectrum of reducing waste and pollutant generation and beneficially recovering, reusing, or recycling what might otherwise become waste. *J. Hirschhorn*

TEOTWAWKI [See "public hearing/meeting"]

teratomobile A monstrously large consumer automobile; an SUV or unnecessarily large truck. *A. Wells* [See "urban assault vehicle"]

terms of venery
A BREAKDOWN of plans. For a term of relatively recent vintage, the expression has achieved wide usage in recent years, and is almost universally applicable today in such expressions as, "The company will shortly issue its latest breakdown of plans." *Anon.*
AN APPOINTMENT of commissioners *R. Stephens*
A BOARD of supervisors *R. Stephens*
A BIG BOX of commercial developers *R. Stephens*

223

A CALCUTTA of panhandlers *J. Lipton*
A COLD SHOLDER of passersby *J. Lipton*
A COMMUNITY of planners *R. Stephens*
A DASH of commuters *J. Lipton*
A DISCORD of experts *J. Lipton*
A DOCKET of cases *J. Lipton*
A DRIFT of lecturers *J. Lipton*
A GROWTH of developers *K. Bash*
AN ELOQUENCE of lawyers *J. Lipton*
AN ESCHEAT of lawyers *J. Lipton*
AN EXAMPLE of masters *J. Lipton*
AN EYESORE of graffiti *J. Lipton* [See "graffiti"]
A FORREST of antennas *J. Lipton* [See "cell tower"]
A GANNT of project managers *SlangSite*
A HASSLE of bureaucrats *R. Bayan*
A HUDDLE of homeless *J. Lipton*
A LATITUDE of maps *J. Lipton*
A LOT of realtors *J. Lipton*
A MAZE of bureaucrats *J. Lipton*
A NERVE of neighbors *J. Lipton*
A PEDRO MENDELBAUM of creative designers *SlangSite*
A PLOT of planners *R. Stephens*
A RENDERING of architects *J. Lipton*
A ROLL of plans *R. Stephens*
A SCHOOL of scholars *J. Lipton*
A SCLEROSIS of fast foods *J. Lipton* [See "restaurant, formula"]
A SPRAWL of malls *J. Lipton* [See "sprawl"]
A STRANGLE of city dwellers *J. Lipton*

224

A SUBDIVISION of builders *R. Stephens*
A TRANSPLANT of suburbanites *J. Lipton* [See "suburbia"]
A TWADDLE of public speakers *J. Lipton*
A VIGILANCE of environmentalists *J. Lipton* [See "environmentalist"]
A WORSHIP of writers *J. Lipton*

terraculture Agriculture. *H.F. Byrne*

territorios inteligentes Smart places. (Spanish) *A. Vegara*

terrorforming Extremely bad urban designing. The opposite of "terraform:" To change a planet's surface and atmosphere so that life as it exists on Earth is possible. *R. Stephens*

tetris tract Subdivision map achieving maximum yield/lotting. *R. Stephens*

theoretical Nobody in their right mind would ever consider building the crazy thing. *Glass Steel and Stone* [See "architecture"]

Thinking Beyond the Pavement (TBTP) [See "context sensitive solutions"]

thinking outside the big box Planning for retail commercial development other than 'big boxes'. *R. Stephens* [See "big box"]

Thor's Hammer Norse god gavel. *R. Stephens*

Three Rules of Ruination [See "engineer" and "rules"]

three-toes-over-the-cliff conservation Last minute efforts to save an animal that is close to extinction. *Anon.*

tilt-up Concrete building constructed by pouring cement into molds on the ground around the foundation, then raising them up to make walls. *Anon.*

tin pan alley An area in a city where the popular-music industry is based. *Probert Eneyclopaedia*

TM Transcendental Meditation. Metaphysical movement of people and goods. (Transportation Management) *H. Eng AICP*

TND Traditional Neighborhood Development with conventional main streets and a small-town atmosphere. *A. Duany*

TOADS Temporarily Obsolete Abandoned Derelict Sites. *F. Popper*

TOD [See "transit-oriented development]

TODZILLA A Transit Oriented Development of inordinate size. *R. Stephens*

TCTC Too Close To Call. A hearing or election outcome that cannot be accurately predicted. *D. Rather*

TLC 1) Total Loss Conditions. Conditions of approval that compromise the physical or economic viability of the project. The opposite of 'tender loving care.' 2) Total Loss of Consciousness. A phenomenon common in public meetings and hearings. 3) Test Laboratory Conditions. Experimental conditions of approval. *R. Stephens*

226

topography, significantly severe Hills. *R. Dymsza.* Horizontally challenged slopes. *J. Harrison*

topolatry Worship of a place. *H.F. Byrne*

topomancy Fortunetelling by the contour of the land. *B. Clark*

toponymy The study of place names and their origins. *G. Clay*

tornado bait One or more mobile homes or trailers, especially when located in or near a tornado zone. *T. Eblen* [See "factory-built home," "trailer parks" and "tornado bait"]

tot lot [See "lot"]

tourismatic Places that arouse fervent popular devotion and enthusiasm. I.e. Las Vegas, Disneyland, etc. (charismatic) *R. Stephens*

town In many parts of Europe it is still unusual to find a farmer who lives upon his farm. Generally he lives in a nearby village and walks each day to his fields. The custom is a survival from olden times when, for the sake of mutual protection at night, men slept within call of others. Their group of houses in those days was surrounded by a tight hedge or fence through which no marauding wild animal could gain access. In Old England this hedge was known as *tun* (pronounced "toon"). Later, *tun* indicated any kind of enclosure, especially, a wall; and eventually it referred more specifically to the place enclosed by such a wall, a walled village. Thus a *town*, of early and Medieval England, was distinguished from a hamlet or a village

227

by virtue of the wall that then surrounded it. *C. Funk*

Town/Gown Split Difference[s] between communities and college/university campuses. *L. Peloquin* [See "studentification"]

town square 1) The traditional center of a town. 2) The clueless elected official. *E.M. Vargas*

tract home [See "house"]

tract mansion [See "mansionization"]

trade dress [See "signage"]

traffic [See "Bruce-Brigg's Law of Traffic" and "Law of Road Construction].

traffic analysis Trying to figure out those personalized license plates. *R. Castillo*

traffic calming devices Speed bumps, traffic islands, rumble strips, etc. that force drivers to slow down. Often used to keep drivers from speeding through quiet neighborhoods or to make selected streets less attractive as alternate routes. *E. Shaw*

traffic circle A circular one-way road at a junction of thoroughfares, facilitating an uninterrupted flow of traffic. Also called rotary (regional) and roundabout (British).

traffic sedatives [See "traffic calming devices"]

traffical Heavy traffic. *Pseudodictionary*

traffic tranquilizing Extreme traffic calming measures. *R. Stephens*

Tragedy of the Commons Much of man's world is treated as a "commons" wherein individuals have the right to freely consume its resources and return their wastes. The "logic of the commons" ultimately produces its ruin as well as the demise of those who depend upon it for survival. Example: The Commons is a shared plot of grassland used by all livestock farmers in a village. Each farmer keeps adding more livestock to graze on the Commons, because he does not experience a direct cost for doing so. In a few years, the soil is depleted by overgrazing, the Commons becomes unusable and the village perishes. *G. Hardin* Anyone questioning this theory has not experienced the "Tragedy of the Office Refrigerator." *R. Stephens*

trail boss Leader of a team of incompetent or crooked builders (cowboys). (British) *Probert Encyclopaedia*

trailer parks 1) Latter-day gypsy camps scattered throughout the vast American hinterland; humble places of abode where aspirations die young and tornadoes gravitate like flies to roadkill. *R. Bayan* 2) Manufactured home facilities. *W. Lutz* [See "factory-built home" and "tornado bait"]

transect [See "rural-urban transect"]

transit-oriented development (TOD) Built around bus or rail lines. *P. Calthorpe*

transitron Traffic signal. *W. Lutz*

transnational suburb [See "suburbia"]

TRAP The Realtor Always Promised. Preface to disappointing assurances regarding property use, adjacent development, and future city improvements. Also, 'houseTRAP.' *R. Stephens* [See "XYZ"]

trash truck treatment [rule of thumb] Place-making based on the requirements and constraints of a trash truck. Roads and alleys must easily accommodate the width of trash trucks and their collection arms. Cul-de-sacs must easily accommodate the turning radius of a trash truck. Grades must not exceed the ability of trash trucks. And so on. *J. Freiman AICP*

tree-hugger [See "environmentalist"]

tree shit Such byproducts of the life cycle of trees as fall to the ground. E.g. leaves, fruit, seed pods, bird excrement. The cleaning up of such detritus is seen as the primary argument, other than cost, for not putting trees in parking lots. *J. Garreau*

trespassage-way A way between two points across someone's land made without their permission or consent. *E.M. Vargas*

trespassing To enter onto another's land wrongfully. Never considered by the general public to include picnicking, riding, hiking, or any recreational use. *E.M. Vargas* [See "squatter's field" and "trespastime"]

trespassion The strong emotions regarding trespassing. *E.M. Vargas*

trespastime Recreation on private property without permission or consent. *E.M. Vargas*

230

triangulation That process by which some external stimulus provides a linkage between people and prompts strangers to talk to each other as though they were not. (The Social Life of Small Urban Spaces) *W.H. Whyte*

tribal mentality Territorial behavior. *D. Walters*

Trifecta [See "Triple Crown"]

Triple Crown Race to receive entitlement with only one design review meeting, one planning commission hearing, and one city council hearing. Also 'hat trick' and 'Trifecta.' *R. Stephens* [See "Iron Plan Triathlon" and "public hearing"]

trolley Shopping cart. (British) *P. Tutt*

Trump variance Use or structure granted that is not permitted in the zone for a significant community member. Example: "Your application for the casino next to the elementary school has been approved. You're wired." *J. Stephens*

turf 1) Area or territory felt to belong to a person or gang. *Probert Encyclopaedia* 2) Landscape spelled out; it says who goes where, who belongs, and who does not; it is admonitory and administered. *G. Clay*

turfing Setting up fences, "keep out" signs, etc. *G. Clay* [See "turf"]

Turismo - Terrorismo Italian pun on the relationship between tourism and [socio-environmental] terrorism. *J. Fest*

turning to the dark side Switching from public sector to private sector planning. *K. Gardner* [See "gone native" and "seeing the light"]

two wind-sock model [See "corporate estate"]

TWOC Taking WithOut Consent. Condemnation. *J. Stephens*

typology The study or systematic classification of types that have characteristics or traits in common. Designer-babble for 'types.' [See "designer-babble"]

U

UED Urban Entertainment Development. *Anon.*

ULI Approved Urban Land Institute blessing. *Anon.*

undulated road Speed bumps. *W. Lutz* [See "traffic calming"]

uni University. *J. Green* [See "institutions"]

unique retail biosphere Farmer's market. *W. Lutz*

universal design A framework for the design of products, environments, and communication to be usable by everyone, to the greatest extent possible, without special or separate design. The concept is also called 'inclusive design,' 'design-for-all' and 'lifespan design.' *Designing for the 21st Century*

university planning departments Historic preservation projects for endangered intellectuals. *Anon.*

unsitely Not able to fit on the site. Example: "The mansionized house was so big, it was unsitely." *R. Stephens*

upsetback Setback for upper stories. *E.M. Vargas*

upzone To *reduce* the intensity of use by decreasing allowable density or lowering the floor area ratio or otherwise increasing bulk requirements. Comment: This phrase, and its counterpart, downzoning, is often misused and has certain class distinctions. It would be more accurate to use terms such as 'more restrictive,' 'less restrictive,' 'more intense,' or 'less intense.' *H. Moskowitz* [See "downzone"]

urban assault vehicle (UAV) New generation of sport utility vehicles designed for the urban jungle. The "Hummer" is the archetype. *R. Stephens* [See "jungle"]

urban aura An exceptionally powerful sense of place. *R. Stephens*

urban design Leftover from paint mixing accident. Let the chips fall where they may. *R. Castillo*

urban fabric The generic term for the physical aspect of urbanism, emphasizing building types, thoroughfares, open space, frontages, and streetscapes; while excluding without prejudice to this useful term, environmental, functional, economic and socio-cultural aspects. *Parole*

urban fabric softener Generic zoning that smoothes out the distinctions between areas. *R. Stephens*

urban front The region outside the city which epitomizes dynamic unrest. The word 'front' enables us to consider these place-processes as zones of unpredictable change, uneasy alliances and standoffs, and active citizen negotiation and treaty making. (military, meteorological) *G. Clay*

urban guerrilla artist 1) Person creating illegal environmental art works such as replacing "WALK/DON'T WALK" flashing street signs with "CONFORM/ CONSUME" and placing foaming detergent in the public fountain. *The Associated Press* 2) Politically correct term for vandal? [See "environmental art" and "graffiti"]

urban legends Urban legends include affordable housing, sewergators, the 40-hr week, brief presentations, etc. *R. Stephens* [See "endangered species"]

urban literacy The capacity to 'read' and understand cities. *C. Landry*

urban removal [See "urban renewal"]

urban renewal 1) The replacement of old inner-city slums with newer, uglier ones. *R. Bayan* Urban renewal is 'urban removal;' an attempt to push problems of the inner city a bit further away to make it more profitable to erect skyscrapers. *P. Johnson*

urban reserve Land destined to be developed. Simultaneously viewed as either all of the land outside the city, or all of the undeveloped lots within the city. *R. Stephens*

urban scatteration Urban sprawl. *R. Dymsza* [See "sprawl"]

urban scene dirty old man Strip development. Also, 'urban/suburban scapegoat.' *G. Clay*

urban software Identity, social development or network dynamics. *C. Landry*

urban surfing Riding on the outside of a moving vehicle. *Probert Encyclopaedia*

urban-tumbleweed The various bits of trash that blow by you in the city on a windy day. *T. Pentacle*

urbanimal [See "animals"]

urbanity The kind of civility that urban observers ascribe to dwellers in all cities but New York. Its commonest expression is heard in the words, "I beg your pardon," and it is not inconsistent with disregard of the rights of others. *A. Bierce*

urbanonymity The strange feeling of anonymity that results from living in a large, densely populated city. *S. Mize*

urbicolous Living in the city. *H.F. Byrne*

utopiary From Utopia—where all is perfect—and topiary—the art of cutting hedges. For a state of slightly mundane perfection in a middle-class housing estate gardening sense. *Pseudodictionary*

V

Valhalla High-tech oasis located in a rural area like Park City, Utah; Jackson Hole, Wyoming; and Aspen, Colorado. *J. Kotkin*

value engineering The process of designing structures so that they can be built as cheaply as possible, usually by systematically eliminating such frivolities as esthetics. *J. Garreau*

vanilla An adjective for a bland or boring design or plan. *C. Chelst* [See "a la mode"]

variance Permission to depart from the literal requirements of a zoning ordinance. [See "Board of Zoning Adjustment"] Repetitive requests are "variances on a theme." [See "Lavelle Amendment"] *M. Multari*

variations on a theme park The new American city and the end of public space. *M. Sorkin*

vasectomy zoning [See "zoning"]

vehicular interaction Automobile accident. *W. Lutz*

velcro planning Planning where land uses are constantly changed according to the market (time and tides, atmospheric changes, and the developer's biorhythm). *T. Day* [See Golf Course Syndrome]

venturi principle Significant small, regional and metropolitan traffic flows that are constricted like a venturi tube and are thereby more intensely active. *G. Clay*

verdicuum [See "house"]

vertically integrated destination resort High rise hotel. *M. Roos AICP*

Vesting Tentative Map Tentative Map conditioned so as to have a vesting right to develop.   Initial Feasibility Studies for these maps are "investing in vesting investigations." [See "initial feasibility studies"]

vicinage A neighborhood, vicinity. *First American Title Company*

viewbicle Cubicle with a view. *Pseudodictionary*

village green [See "environmentalists"]

ville nouvelle New towns. *F. Rapinat*

Vintages & Vinegar, Oranges & Lemons, Orchids & Onions, Wine & Sour Grapes...
Awards programs recognizing excellent <u>and</u> poor environmental design. *R. Stephens*

vision A mystical force guiding one to Utopia. *R. Castillo* [See "General Plan"]

La vista tanque farme A property with soaring, panoramic views of largely industrial areas. *K. Bradfield*

volleyball court analogy [See "sport analogies"]

volume reduction plant Dump. *W. Lutz*

volumetric expression Really big and boxy building. *M. Roos AICP* [See "B4 and after"]

voodoo Elaborate text. *M. Beach*

Vorpal Sword (Alice in Wonderland) X-acto blade wielded by a graphics expert. (graphics) *R. Stephens* [See "Excalibur"]

VPL Visible Property Line. A fence or other feature that shows the property boundary. Example: We could see the VPL on the aerial photo by the difference in landscape. (visible panty line) *R. Stephens*

W

walk-up A multistory apartment building that does not have an elevator. Sometimes used synonymously with *tenement*—a run down building without the amenities, or *cold-water flat*, both indicating a generally deteriorated apartment. D.E. *Miller*

Wally World The largest big box chain in the world. (WalMart) *S. Nugget* [See "big box"]

waltzing the developer   Delays and additional information requests for the developer from public agencies. [Different jurisdictions have different dances]. *A. Davies*

watch analogy View of the environment as a wristwatch. You can remove a piece here and there, and it will still work until you remove a piece that stops everything. This 'mechanical model' of the world has long since been replaced with a 'systems model' by most scientists. *R. Stephens* [See "First Law of Tinkering"]

waterpark resort A destination-esque resort which will include an indoor waterpark complex, as may include waterslides and water-play areas; may or may not include a wavepool among its distractions. Originated in Wisconsin Dells, circa 1990, which happens to have 16 such. *K. Accidentale*

weapon of mass construction Suburban sprawl. *C. Chipping*

weapon of mass distraction Something that distracts large numbers of people from thinking about important issues. *M. Landsberg* [See "petition proliferation"]

weasel words A Condition of Approval that incorporates intentional verbal padding or vagueness in order to evade direct commitment. Usually designed to appease one party while allowing another party to "weasel out," if current events, financial hardship, the political climate, etc. so dictate. Example: "The Save the Weasels program shall be carried out to the maximum extent feasible, if determined to be necessary by the Director." *L. Phillips AICP*

wetlands 1) Noxious swamp. *R. Blewett* 2) The marshy wilderness frequented by ducks, the hunters who shoot them, the environmentalists who lecture the hunters, and the condominium developers who inevitably outfox them all. *R. Bayan* [See "greenwash," "jungle," "nonwetlands" and "squish test"]

what the traffic will bear An excessive but obtainable traffic mitigation fee. *R. Stephens*

wheel estate Mobile homes. *A. Wallis* [See "factory-built home"]

Where's my house? There's my house! The two most common responses to aerial photographs. *R. Stephens* [See "Lilliput Syndrome"]

whistle stop [See "rural country"]

white acre A fanciful name for a hypothetical piece of land, esp. in lawbooks to distinguish one piece of land from another. *L. Urdang* [See "black acre"]

white-breadroom community [See "bedroom community"]

white painter [See "brick sniffers"]

wide-body lot [See "lot"]

WIIFM [See "nimbyism"]

wilderness area Primary source of the raw material for junk mail, supermarket tabloids, romance novels, user's manuals, toilet tissue and this dictionary. *R. Bayan*

wildlife conservation park [See "zoo"]

wildlife preserves New product line from the Smuckers Company. *M. Roos AICP* [See "zoo"]

wind farm A collection of generators that convert wind power into electricity. *J. Kerr*

windbaggery An airy form of packaging dear to chambers of commerce and tourism promoters. *G. Clay*

windfalls and wipeouts External economies and diseconomies. Beneficial and detrimental externalities. Winners and losers. *A. Davies*

window dressing [See "architectural ornamentation" and "fenestration"]

windshield survey When the planner drives by and actually looks at the site he/she is writing about. *J. Parnell AICP*

wireless telecommunications facility [See "cell tower"]

Wizard of Laws City attorney. *J. Stephens*

WNK [See "animals"]

Wolf's Planning Law A good place to start from is where you are. *C. Wolf*

WOMBAT Waste Of Money, Brains And Time. *D. Hauptman*

wonk To answer a question or criticism with a technical, detailed, brainy response, which suggests nothing but expertise on the subject. *K. Watts*

Wood's Law The more unworkable the urban plan, the greater the probability of implementation. *R. Wood* [See "assumptions"]

woody-goody theme [See "architectural style"]

woonerf The Dutch term *woonerf* refers to a narrow street in which cars move slowly because they share the space with pedestrians. *R. E. Knack* [See "traffic calming"]

wordsmith A very skilled writer. *Anon.*

workforce housing Politically acceptable alternative to 'affordable housing.' *Anon.* [See "affordable housing"]

World Town Planning Day (WTPD) November 8th is recognized by numerous countries as 'World Town Planning Day.' *International Society of City and Regional Planners*

wrinkle ranch A name used in place of nursing home, senior citizen estates, and so forth. *Pseudodictionary* [See "NORC" and "raisin ranch"]

X

xenophobia Fear of change not to be confused with 'fear of Amazonian warriors'. *Anon.*

xeriscape A new term that developers think means "zeroscape" or no landscaping in their projects. *Dear Mary, The Dispatch* [Landscape consisting primarily of species and practices which require little or no maintenance, watering or fertilization.]

X-Men Graphic experts with x-acto knives, Excalibur, and xylene markers. *R. Stephens* [See "Excalibur" and "xylene queen"]

xylene queen 'Graphic artist' from the old marker carcinogen. *B. Lewis* [See "inkslinger" and "X-Men"]

XYZ Examine Your Zone. Advice never given by realtors to prospective buyers regarding home additions, neighboring permitted uses, property restrictions, etc. *R. Stephens* [See "TRAP"]

Y

yahoomanity People en masse. *H.F. Byrne*

yard garbage The tacky stuff that people use to "decorate" their yards: wooden sheep covered in wool, windmills made from soda bottles, plastic animals, cartoon of a woman bending over gardening….and don't forget to mention gnomes. *R.M. Wilson* [See "lawn ornaments"]

yellow stuff Heavy equipment used for grading and construction. (military) [See "drop some iron"] *Anon.*

yield 1) Number of units a project can create. 2) Most commonly heard request/demand. *C. Chipping* [See "density"]

yoghurt cities [See "city"]

yuppie [See "demographics"]

yuppie slum A neighborhood with older and slightly run-down houses that young professionals purchase and renovate.   *J. Clarke*

Z

zanzibarian Bearing a resemblance to the town of Zanzibar in Tanzania. Small and charming, with lots of little cobbled streets between old buildings with huge and ornate doors. *C. Hansson*

ZEN Zone of Exceptional Novelty. A zone that is written for a very specific use or user. *R. Stephens* [See "ZOA" and "ZOT!"]

Zen of Place That moment of insight when you know you have arrived: sense of place satori. *R. Stephens*

zero lot [See "lot"]

zero lot line 1) A very cold lot line. *R. Reitzel* 2) Condition where a building abuts a property line. *K. Watts*

zipper lot [See "lot"]

ZOA Zoning Ordinance Anachronisms. Those small organisms from an earlier time that inhabit zoning ordinances. The obsolete words and expressions from the old ordinance that were never revised or replaced. *R. Stephens*
Examples include:
- billiard parlor (replaced by 'pool hall')
- blueprinting service (replaced by 'photocopier service')

- cobbler shop (replaced by 'shoe store')
- confectionery (candy store)
- dance hall (replaced by 'discothèque')
- diner (often replaced by fastfood or netcafé)
- discothèque (follow up from 'dance hall')
- drive-in theater
- drygoods store (textiles or clothing store)
- gutta percha manufacturing (product similar to rubber and used by dentists to make temporary fillings)
- emporium (marketplace)
- haberdashery shop (men's clothing store)
- malt shop (replaced by 'coffee shop' then replaced by 'coffee stores' i.e. *Starbucks*)
- millinery shop (women's hat shop)
- mimeographing service (replaced by 'photocopier service')
- mobile home (replaced with "manufactured home") [See "factory-built home"]
- nickelodeon (replaced by 'movie theater')
- notions and sundries (small lightweight items for household use)
- pool hall (follow up from 'billiard parlor')
- service station (replaced by the "self-serve" gas station)
- sex shop (replaced with retro 'intimacy salon')
- soda fountain (replaced by 'coffee store')
- telegram/telegraph service (replaced by 'Internet cafés')
- typewriter repair shop (replaced by computer stores)
- video game arcade (replaced by 'Internet game centers)

ZOMBIE   Zoning Ordinance Maintained By Inert Employees. A lifeless, soulless zoning code. *R. Stephens*

zone/zoning 1) Common zones within a planning department include demilitarized [DMZ], erogenous, and twilight. *R. Stephens* 2) The zoning laws in most American neighborhoods would not *permit* the construction of a Parthenon [Lichtenberg's Insight]. *B. Lichtenberg* 3) Local ordinances that typically prohibit commercial construction adjacent to bird sanctuaries or family dwellings, at least until a wealthy developer proposes a $500 million shopping mall for the site. *R. Bayan* [See "McClaughry's Iron Law of Zoning]

ACREAGE ZONING Zoning designed to reduce residential density by requiring larger lot sizes. Also known as "Snob Zoning". *Kenneth Leventhal & Company*

AESTHETIC ZONING The regulation of building or site design to achieve desirable appearance. *APA*

AREA ZONING Mainly residential zoning which regulates the ratio of improvements to land, setbacks, etc. Also called 'bulk zoning.' *Real Estate Dictionary*

AZONIC Not local; not restricted to a particular zone. *L. Urdang*

COMBAT ZONE Sleazy, dirty and, at times, violent set of downtown streets. *Parole*

DMZ 1) Street or area of a city that demarks high-crime area from one with average or low crime rate. (De-Militarized Zone) *P. Dickson* 2) Dangerous Movement Zone. Highways that are traveled by heavy trucks posing a threat to automobiles. *G. Clay*

DOWNZONE 1) The battle cry of a population sick of growth and its negative attributes. Downzoning is that method by which the amount of development in an area is reduced, by decreasing the legally allowable density. By spreading development farther apart, Downzoning often has ironic effects—such as increasing the need for automobiles, hence creating traffic congestion, which decreases the Quality of Life that Downzoning was originally meant to advance. But for the purposes of the groups advocating this remedy, that is generally beside the point. Since there are few other effective legal methods currently available to fight growth,

246

they go with what they've got. And Downzoning does increase developer's costs—thereby having a genuine effect on growth. *J. Garreau* 2) To **increase** the intensity of use by increasing density or floor area ratio or otherwise decreasing bulk requirements. Comment: Developers and some landowners consider this term to have the opposite meaning. *H. Moskowitz* 3) A change in the allowable use of land by the appropriate zoning authority to a lesser (usually less valuable) use. Example: Eight units per acre to four units per acre. *Real Estate Dictionary*

EARTH TONE ZONE Suburban residential area. *R. Stephens* [See "earth tones"]

EUCLIDEAN ZONING Categorizing and segregating land uses so everyone's lives are spent traveling from place to place. There is no connection with Euclidean geometry. The name is from the 1926 Euclid v. Ambler Realty Co. Supreme Court decision. *R. Stephens*

GOD'S GREEN ACRES Large lot zoning, especially as opposed to multi-family zoning. *R. Stephens*

HOME ZONE A home zone is a residential street where the living environment clearly predominates over any provision for traffic. The design provides space for motor vehicles, but fully accommodates the wider needs of residents. This is achieved by adopting approaches to street design, landscaping and highway engineering that control how vehicles move without restricting the number of vehicular movements. *M. Biddulph*

ISLAND ZONING [See "zone/zoning, spot zoning"]

NO ZONE, THE Any place that is bad to be. *Ditnis*

OH-ZONE Redlight district. *J. Marquez*

PAINTING THE TOWN RED Commercial zone changes. *R. Stephens* [See "color code/convention"]

PERFORMANCE ZONING Describing what is wanted rather than what is not wanted.

PYRAMID ZONING Including more restrictive uses in less restrictive uses.

Examples: Residential use [more restrictive] would be allowed in an area zoned commercial [less restrictive]; commercial [more restrictive] would be allowed in an area zoned industrial [less restrictive]. *First American Title Co*

ROBIN HOOD METHOD Inclusionary Zoning to provide low-cost housing. *B. Inman*

SNOB ZONING [See "zone/zoning, acreage zoning"]

SPOT ZONING A small area devoted to an isolated land use—often commercial.

VASECTOMY ZONING Zoning laws and other restrictions that aim to keep children out of an area or neighborhood. *D. Magnani* [See "architectural birth control"]

ZONING FOR DOLLARS The practice of zoning excessive amounts of higher valued industrial and commercial land in the hopes of improving fiscal balance. *R. Stephens*

Zone Ranger, The 'Who was that masked planner?' *R. Stephens* [See "administrative guerilla"]

zoning balance the twin needs for 'flexibility' and 'certainty.' *P. Crawford AICP*

Zoning Czar/Czarina Planning Director, "Ruler of All the Rushes. *R. Stephens*

zoning geek Planner devoted to zoning issues. *P. Crawford AICP*

zoning ordinance anachronisms [See "ZOA"]

zoning ordinance taboo [See "ZOT!"]

zoning map

BRITISH	zoning plan
GERMAN	Flächennutzungsplan

FRENCH	plan de occupation des sold (POS)
ITALIAN	piano di zonizzazione
SPANISH	plan de zonificación

zoo (zoological garden) 1) A pleasant and instructive wildlife park, lately denounced for depriving animals of their right to starve or be eaten alive in their natural habitats. *R. Bayan* 2) Wildlife conservation program with some permanent facilities. *W. Lutz* 2) A mall or other multiplex shopping facility, where most of the animals on display are miserable and insane, yet wouldn't last a day without the assistance of their retail captors. *DDX*

ANIMALCATRAZ From 'animal' and 'Alcatraz' prison. *J. Stephens*

MEGAZOO Concept of the world as a place where animals are kept for public exhibition. *A Sullivan*

WILDLIFE CONSERVATION PARK *W. Conway*.

WILDLIFE CONSERVATION PROGRAM WITH SOME PERMANENT FACILITIES *W. Lutz*

WILDLIFE PRESERVATION CENTER [See "wildlife preserves"]

ZULAG From 'zoo' and 'gulag' *H. Beard.*

ZUTOPIA Zoo where predators and prey co-exist in artificial harmony. It would spoil the kids' day at the zoo to see how a lion would actually behave around a zebra. *R. Stephens* [See "greenwash"]

ZOO Zoning Ordinance Outfit. Planning department. [See "Board of Zoning Adjustment"] *R. Stephens*

ZORRO Zoning Ordinance Regulating Residential Occupations. ZORROs free the people from the tyranny of Euclidean zoning. *R. Stephens* [See "Euclidean Zoning"]

ZOT! Zoning Ordinance Taboo. The various incompatible land uses that the public wishes to smite. Sometimes referred to as an "unsavory business" or "adverse land use." *R. Stephens* [See "combatible," "LULU," "nimbyism" and "SCRUB"]

Examples include:

- 99-cent store
- automotive stereo store with on-site installation
- billiard parlor / pool hall
- cell tower [See "cell tower"]
- check cashing store
- convenience store
- crematorium/mortuary
- dump (sanitary landfill)
- liquor store
- massage parlor
- mental institution [See "institution"]
- pawn shop
- prison [See "institution"]
- sexually oriented business [See "SOB"]
- smoke shop
- tattoo parlor
- taxidermist
- video/Internet arcade

Zulag [See "zoo"]

zygocephalum In civil law an inaccurate measure of land. The area of land a yoke of oxen could plow in one day. *First American Title Company*

Note: The Plannerese Dictionary omits the Congressional Panel on Obscenity's list of "almost dirty" words— *adulterate, Balzac, capitulate, cockatoo, combustible, consommé, copious, crotchety, dickey, erroneous, fallacious, hot cross buns, laity, luster, masticate, penal, rapier, screwdriver, sects, spurn, and titular*.

First Printing [500] March 1991
Second Printing [500] July 1991
Third Printing [500] March 1992
Fourth Printing [200] August 1993
Fifth Printing [300] September 1994
There's just no telling how many copies have been printed since 1994...

Richard Bryan Stephens is a consulting planner with over 25 years experience in master-planned community, resort & tourism, information technology & communications, and international planning. Ric is an adjunct university professor; editor/webmaster for several professional organizations; airport and city planning commissioner; and advisor to several international organizations. Ric and his wife, June, enjoy horseback wilderness trekking, sailing, and flying.

Please send examples of Plannerese to:

Richard B. Stephens
4520 Champagne Court
Riverside California 92505
USA

ISBN 1-41204794-3

Printed in the United States
By Bookmasters